Ron Sisk's *Right and Wrong* has two major strengths. The first is the way it parses contemporary culture's ethical challenges in the context of a commitment to classic Christian values rooted in *agape*. The second is its encouragement to pursue a way to think about ethical issues without attempting to mandate a singular response. Sisk's method and content will remind readers of Rilke's wise encouragement to "live the questions."

—*Richard F. Wilson*
Emeritus Professor of Religion
Mercer University

Smyth & Helwys Publishing, Inc.
6316 Peake Road
Macon, Georgia 31210-3960
1-800-747-3016
©2023 by Ronald D. Sisk
All rights reserved.

Library of Congress Cataloging-in-Publication Data on file

RIGHT
AND
WRONG

Finding Values for the 21st Century

RONALD D. SISK

Also by *Ronald D. Sisk*

Surviving Ministry

The Competent Pastor:
Skills and Self-Knowledge for Serving Well

Preaching Ethically:
Being True to the Gospel, Your Congregation & Yourself

To Sheryl and Doug,
who make me want to get it right.

Acknowledgments

No book is written by oneself. Even though I began this writing almost as an act of defiance in the midst of the isolation of the pandemic lockdown, my wife Sheryl offered her usual listening ear and honest feedback from the beginning. Longtime friend and weekly correspondent the Rev. Dr. Michael A. Smith provided an editor's eye as the chapters accumulated. He was the first to say, "I think you might have a useful book here." Despite the changes in the publishing world in recent years, he encouraged me to continue believing in the project as potentially useful for Sunday school classes and discussion groups as well as students of Christian ethics.

Thanks are also due to my pastor, the Rev. Dr. Corey Nelson at First Presbyterian Church of Fort Collins, Colorado, and the retired pastors' group there who were some of the first to read the manuscript for me, as well as various mentors, friends, and colleagues who graciously accepted out-of-the-blue requests to read the manuscript. My lifelong friend Mitch paid me perhaps the highest compliment when he allowed out of his very different perspective that what I was saying actually made sense.

Thanks go to a generation of students at Sioux Falls Seminary whose hunger for truth kept me perennially on my intellectual toes. And thanks are due to the people of the four churches who put up with me as their pastor: Forks of Elkhorn Baptist Church, Midway, Kentucky; Tiburon Baptist Church, Tiburon, California; Western Hills Baptist Church, Ft. Worth, Texas; and Crescent Hill Baptist Church, Louisville, Kentucky. Together they taught me that the Gospel is about loving people where and as they are.

Of course this book would not have happened without Keith Gammons, Smyth & Helwys's publisher, who decided that if I believed so strongly in the project, he would believe in it too. And enormous thanks are due to book editor Leslie Clugston Andres, who made it her mission to hold my feet to the fire on the details of production. And, finally, thanks to that fearless prophet and original thinker the late Henlee Hulix Barnette. Dr. Barnette zeroed in on the Gospel's profound and beautiful simplicity and made it the work of a lifetime. I owe him more than I could ever say.

Loveland, Colorado
August 2023

Contents

Foreword

After forty-five years as a Christian minister, pastor, and seminary professor, I've become convinced that one of the chief problems thoughtful Christians have is how to interact with the challenges of everyday life in a way that is reasonable, realistic, and faithful. When the Covid pandemic hit the United States in early 2020, I, like many others (especially in my age group), found myself isolating at home with little to do beyond keeping up with the media and thinking about how the nation was responding to the myriad economic, political, and public health challenges we were all facing together.

I found myself going back to a relatively simple approach I had learned in Christian ethics class as a seminarian. As the pandemic continued and issues succeeded one another in the headlines, I found myself writing down how that simple approach, grounded in a particular definition of the primary New Testament term for Christian love—*agape*—and taught in that Christian ethics class by Dr. Henlee H. Barnette, remains both intellectually and spiritually robust enough to serve as a guide for Christians and others of good will.

I offer this little book in the hope that you will find this approach as useful in your life as I have found it in mine.

—*Ron Sisk*
Loveland, Colorado
Valentine's Day, 2023

Chapter 1

How We Got This Way

Everybody faces the question sooner or later. "What is the right thing to do?"

Woodrow Wilson, the intellectual Presbyterian from segregationist Virginia, is supposed to have said, "The South is the only place in the world where I never have to ask any questions." What he meant was that the American South of his upbringing was a place of moral and cultural certainty. Everybody who was anybody was a white Protestant Christian, at least in name. Black people were tolerated as long as they kept to their assigned subordinate place. America's founding principles were venerated as long as they weren't applied too stringently to the concrete interactions of everyday life. In Wilson's world, the guiding assumptions of behavior didn't have to be discussed because the vast majority of people believed they were right. This was how life ought to be lived. Anyone who didn't adhere to that belief was either an "uppity" Black person, a ne'er-do-well, or, worst of all, a Yankee.

That world was largely myth. It was never genuine. But growing up in Arkansas in the Deep South of the 1950s and 1960s, I absorbed the power and the perversion of that myth with the very air I breathed. At the same time, from the day I sat in front of our tiny black and white television at age seven and watched the first African American students make their nervous way into Little Rock's Central High School, some inarticulate thing in me began to wonder how keeping them out could possibly be the right thing for us white folks to do. From my earliest venture into Sunday school as a first grader at Mount Pleasant Baptist Church, the culture of the United States has become the fascination of a lifetime. I've spent a long career trying to understand both the spoken and unspoken rules of our culture in the second half of the twentieth century and into the twenty-first.

Those rules participate in the crisis of authority that grips American life as we move into the third decade of the new century. In his seminal work on American anti-intellectualism, Tom Nichols writes,

> The creation of a vibrant intellectual and scientific culture in the West and in the United States required democracy and secular tolerance. Without such virtues, knowledge and progress fall prey to ideological, religious, and populist attacks. Nations that have given in to such temptations have suffered any number of terrible fates, including mass repression, cultural and material poverty, and defeat in war.[1]

Nichols was writing primarily about the attack on scientific and political knowledge in the United States, but his argument applies equally well to religious and cultural authority. We live in a "do your own thing, do what makes you feel good" world. In the same pages from Nichols's book, he suggests, "I suspect that a possible resolution will lie in a

---

1. *The Death of Expertise* (New York: Oxford University Press, 2017), 236–37.

disaster as yet unforeseen. It may be a war or an economic collapse . . . . It may be in the emergence of an ignorant demagoguery . . . ." He wrote at the beginning of Donald Trump's rise to power in the United States, years before Covid-19 and the consequent recession of 2020. His prescience, though, brings us directly to the moment when I sit down to begin, in late summer 2020, what I hope will become a helpful book on making ethical decisions in twenty-first-century America.

Every hour of every day, the news cycle brings us word of new breaches of long-held norms and new challenges to the political, religious, and cultural ideals that have formed and shaped American life for almost three centuries. Traditional religious authorities seem mired in scandal, threatened by the bogus certainties offered by extremists, or simply irrelevant. The Trump administration daily challenges cherished civic norms and constitutional government in the service of its quest for authoritarian power. The legitimate aspirations of ethnic and social minorities for equality and freedom in everyday life frighten traditionalists and create a backlash against every attempt to move the country forward. Self-indulgence and reluctance to sacrifice even the most trivial individual freedom temporarily for the common good abound. They exacerbate tensions and gaps between generations, political parties, the public itself, and those on whom we depend for safety in times of emergency. Large numbers of Americans this summer have refused even to wear a face mask in public to help protect themselves and others from transmission of a deadly virus. They say they do this to assert their "freedom." As I write, Ruth Bader Ginsburg has just died. Republicans tie themselves in moral knots attempting to explain why it was right to block Barack Obama from appointing a new justice in the election year of 2016 and why it would be wrong to do so in 2020. Democrats interpret the same words in the Constitution to mean exactly the opposite.

In short, as much as any time in living memory, we seem to have lost our way. We struggle to discern the difference between right and wrong. The remainder of this work will be one man's attempt to suggest a practical way forward. In so doing, I write from a particular perspective. I certainly do not claim that it is the only legitimate or best way. Though I can't attain the cosmic spiritual certainties of C. S. Lewis or the quirky eloquence of Frederick Buechner, I seek, at least, to imitate their honesty. And I pray that the reader will find these ideas useful.

The first step in attempting to decide where we as Americans can reclaim some kind of generally acceptable moral grounding is to develop a rudimentary picture of how we got this way. The answer to that is different for each of us. I, for example, occupy what I recognize to be a relatively small subset of American culture.

Without belaboring my own history too much, let me explain. I am the third of five children of a union electrician and a housewife/office worker from the American Southwest. Both my parents were children of the Depression. Both were from large families who were dirt poor. Both of their fathers were alcoholics, with all the family dynamics such an addition entails. Both were high school graduates. They met and married as they finished high school less than a year before the outbreak of World War II. Dad's family was nominally Methodist. Mother's was Primitive Baptist.

The war quickly took them out of their west Texas upbringings. Dad went with the Navy to the Pacific. Mother migrated to Indianapolis to work in the war factories there. Like almost everyone in their generation, they bought into the assurance that America's destiny was to save the world from the Nazis and the Japanese. What the sociologists call their "first adult experience" as part of that conflagration set their worldview in ways that never changed.

By the time I came along within two days of the middle of the century, our family had settled more or less comfortably into the cultural assumptions of working-class evangelical Christianity. Christianity was the only true religion. Baptists were the only true faith. White Southern Baptists were the only believers who had it right. Dad never quite bought into all this, but Mother took the lead in church life.

I have spent my entire adult life attempting to understand that upbringing and the mindset it engenders. The emerging statistics from the losing side of the 2020 election give one cause to believe that this mindset is far more robust and influential than I ever imagined.

Since I hold four academic degrees—a BA in history and political science, an MA in American social history, an MDiv, and a PhD in Christian ethics and church history—my life experience places me in many ways on the cultural boundary between Red and Blue America. I'm an essentially orthodox trinitarian Christian with a progressive understanding of the gospel. As such, I believe deeply that both sides of our current social, political, and theological divides are failing to recognize the essential elements necessary to move us forward as individuals and as a nation.

In brief, broad strokes, the Republican move to the right seems to have begun in the early 1970s, in part as a reaction to the civil rights era and its subsequent embodiment in legislation and in Supreme Court decisions such as *Roe v. Wade*. Republican activists realized early on that the emerging demographic strength of minorities meant that white dominance in American culture was likely being permanently eroded. They also realized that substantial elements of white society around the country lived with a sense of resentment over their perceived loss of privilege and control. And apparently, as exemplified by southern leaders such as George Wallace and Texas judge Paul Pressler, many of them realized they could make common cause with the genuine piety and social conservatism of evangelicals and conservative Catholics.

Over the next thirty years, Republicans worked hard to position themselves not only as the traditional party of business but also as the party of social, political, and religious conservatism, fighting the good fight for traditional America against the forces of secularism and social change. Nowhere was that fight exemplified better than in the perennial efforts at both the state and national levels to limit, eviscerate, and overturn *Roe v. Wade*. The ongoing Republican crusade to install conservative judges on the federal bench took its root and much of its energy from that crusade.

At the same time, both traditional Roman Catholicism and the mainline Protestant churches were losing their hold over the American religious imagination. Catholicism abandoned Latin for worship in the vernacular. American Catholicism, particularly, began to look for ways to become more culturally attractive as Catholics moved more and more into the mainstream. Beginning in the 1960s and becoming more and more dominant as the new century approached, conservative Protestantism abandoned its traditional forms of worship for a more relaxed, informal, emotionally charged expression. Organs gave way to praise bands. Denominational labels gave way to carefully marketed megachurches anchored by preachers with charismatic personalities. Many churches, both Catholic and Protestant, that previously had extensive ties in both political parties began for socially conservative reasons to move more in the direction of Republicanism.

Democrats, for their part, seemed to become more the party of intellectualism, secularism, minority rights, and urban popular culture. As the champions of individual civil rights, they became more strongly identified with causes such as the protection of voting rights, abortion rights, LGBTQ rights, the environment, and the whole range of causes associated with liberalism in late twentieth and early twenty-first-century America.

One result of this polarization was that members of both parties developed cartoonish generalizations with regard to the other group's belief and practice. When Hillary Clinton, for example, described some members of the Republican party as "deplorables" during the 2016 election season, many Republicans took her impolitic reference to a relatively few right-wing extremists as a bigoted description of the mainstream conservatives most saw themselves to be. I remember one thoroughly middle-class couple at my gym who were so offended by Clinton's phrase that they never heard another word she said the entire season. By the same token, many blue-collar working-class Democrats across the country resented Republican characterizations of them as effete intellectual snobs and atheists.

This growing tendency to demonize one another had the unfortunate effect of being a relatively efficient tool for getting partisans of both groups out to the polls. The other guys weren't just mistaken on policy; they were bad, evil, un-American, a danger to the very foundations of the Republic. In the election just past (November 2020), I heard of more threats to leave the country or take up arms if one's side lost than at any other point in a long American life.

This tribalism is not only a danger to the Republic but also presents a serious danger to our basic moral assumptions as a nation. Almost six months after I wrote the previous paragraph, the new administration and the accelerating recovery from the pandemic have done nothing to increase my optimism about the state of our body politic. If anything, the continuing refusal of an intractable minority to view the election itself as legitimate and to credit the scientific/medical community with knowing what they're doing in fighting the virus only make our need for a viable twenty-first-century moral compact even more urgent.

Therefore, what I hope to offer in this book is a relatively simple template, grounded in Judeo-Christian ethical teaching but also both adaptable for and acceptable to a much broader philosophical and religious audience. In short, I'd like to offer what I believe to be a groundwork for a way of ethical thinking that can serve an increasingly secular and humanistic American society as well as satisfy the religiously grounded sensibilities of those who look for a moral framework anchored in either the Abrahamic or the Asian traditions. That is a tall, perhaps impossible, order. Any such effort must necessarily gloss over much of the mythology and specificity of many traditions. But we have nothing to lose and potentially a great deal to gain by giving it a try. In the pages ahead, I will set out my thesis and follow that with specific examples of how that thesis might work to begin to address a selection of the moral challenges of our day.

Questions for Discussion and Reflection

1. Briefly describe your own background and upbringing. What did your nuclear family consist of? Where did you grow up? What did your father, if you grew up with one, do for a living? Did your mother work outside the home? Was your family churched or unchurched as you grew up, or were you from a different religious tradition or none at all? How did your upbringing shape your adult view of right and wrong?

2. This chapter's characterization of the American political scene in recent years may strike you as correct or incorrect in any number of ways. Without assigning blame to one side or another, see if you can describe your own perspective on how we got where we find ourselves as a nation as you begin your journey through this book.

3. In Aristotle's discussions of rhetoric, he says audiences listen from three basic perspectives. Some people listen for *facts*. They want reasonable, logical arguments based as much as possible on reality. Some listen for *passion*. They want to be touched, inspired, and persuaded by a speaker's conviction and certainty. Finally, some listen based on their *personal identification and relationship* with the speaker. They listen because they trust the one speaking. Of these three ways of listening, which do you think is most important for you?

4. When you have already formed an opinion on a given subject, what does it take for you to change your mind? Can you name a time when you have done so?

Chapter 2

Searching for Guiding Principles

In April 1992, three white LAPD officers were acquitted of criminal charges in the beating of Rodney King, whom they had arrested on DUI charges in 1991. That acquittal sparked riots in Los Angeles. In a public statement, King himself asked the question, "Can we all get along?"[2] As a nation, we've been searching for an answer to his question ever since.

In some ways, the problem in searching for meaningful guiding principles that reasonable Americans might agree on in the first quarter of the twenty-first century is that we simply have too many options. A quick list of the various loci of authority currently practiced in the United States includes but is not limited to Judaism; Christianity in its Catholic, Orthodox, Protestant, Evangelical, and Sectarian expressions; Islam; Buddhism; Hinduism; Atheism; Humanism; Capitalism; Socialism; Democracy; Tribalism; Hedonism; and a host of other political, social, and antisocial ideologies.

---

2. Rodney King's LA Riots Speech, May 1, 1992, youtube.com/watch?v=tVidK2kagPA (accessed August 2, 2023).

In a nation of some 330 million souls, each of the above is followed by millions of people. Many of us attempt to follow more than one of these allegiances without even realizing what we're doing. And reports that church membership in 2020 fell below 50 percent for the first time in recent memory suggest that many of our old allegiances are weakening.[3] Often we maintain lip service to an ideology without a clear idea of what authority we're following when we make a given decision.

It's easy, for example, to make a decision believing that you're doing so for one reason while quite another set of influences is at work. With reference to the 2020 presidential election, a substantial percentage of Republicans came to believe that Donald Trump lost to Joe Biden because of widespread election fraud. Many with a substantial loyalty to President Trump simply believed what he said. Others in the evangelical community were told by their pastors that Trump was God's candidate in the election, destined by heaven to win. Many white Republicans carried a deep suspicion of the Democrats as the party of Blacks, Hispanics, LGBTQ people, and uncontrolled immigrants. QAnon and other such conspiracy theories propagated online lent a quasi-religious apocalyptic character to these fears. They felt in the election an existential threat to their own "traditional" American way of life. They couldn't believe the simple fact that Biden won fairly because that belief challenged so many of their most deeply held preferences and assumptions. Even

---

3. Jeffrey M. Jones, "U.S. Church Membership Falls Below Majority for First Time," March 29, 2021, Gallup, news.gallup.com/poll/341963/church-membership-falls-below-majority-first-time.aspx (accessed July 15, 2023).

long after the election, some continued to beat the drum for a triumphant return to office by Trump.[4]

But American confusion is not merely political or simply religious. It is broadly cultural as well. Our contemporary do-what-feels-good-to-you individualism leaves us broadly reluctant to acknowledge traditional ties that have worked to knit us together as a nation. When the coronavirus pandemic broke out, medical authorities like Dr. Anthony Fauci of the National Institute for Health quickly began to call for universal mask-wearing in public as one way of mitigating the spread. What seemed to be a relatively simple, commonsense, science-based precaution quickly provoked unprecedented widespread backlash. Some saw the request as an unwarranted breach of personal freedoms. Others saw it as some sort of darker conspiracy seeking to assert a kind of mind control over the public. Still others reacted against images of Asians wearing masks as though the request was somehow racially motivated. Some evangelicals even associated mask-wearing with the apocalyptic "mark of the beast" image from the book of Revelation. Some Republican congresspeople incurred substantial fines for violating House rules requiring that masks be worn on the floor of the House of Representatives.[5] Jurisdictions across the nation struggled

---

4. Ben Kamisar, "Almost a third of Americans still believe the 2020 election result was fraudulent," June 30, 2023, NBC News, *Meet the Press* blog, nbcnews.com/meet-the-press/meetthepressblog/almost-third-americans-still-believe-2020-election-result-was-fraudule-rcna90145 (accessed July 15, 2023).

5. Kevin B. O'Reilly, "Dr. Fauci outlines 5 ways to blunt COVID-19 pandemic's resurgence," August 4, 2020, American Medical Association, ama-assn.org/delivering-care/public-health/dr-fauci-outlines-5-ways-blunt-covid-19-pandemic-s-resurgence (accessed July 15, 2023); Sarah McCammon, "'Love Your Neighbor' and Get the Shot: White Evangelical Leaders Push COVID Vaccines," April 4, 2021, NPR.com, *All Things Considered*, npr.org/2021/04/05/984322992/love-your-neighbor-

over whether to make masks mandatory in public settings such as restaurants, bars, and stores. Enforcement became a nightmare. Only corporate decisions from national chains such as Walmart to require the masks for entry to their stores provided a modicum of uniformity and acceptance for the precaution across the nation. Even then, as weekly Walmart shoppers living in a relatively compliant jurisdiction, we saw plenty of examples of those, who for whatever reason, refused to comply.

Clearly, we lacked a common value or set of values on which to base and carry out such a decision. And the mask question was only one of a host of issues addressed in piecemeal fashion across the nation. Who should get the Covid vaccines first once they became available? Should they go first to those who were most vulnerable to serious disease and death? What about medical workers and other first responders? What about teachers? College students? Restaurant workers? The military? Some even said we should forget precautions and allow infections to spread broadly, hoping to reach post-infection "herd" immunity as quickly as possible. Black Americans factored in their own historic experience of abuse as guinea pigs by medical researchers studying syphilis. Native Americans dealt with their longstanding suspicion of the motives of the United States government. Those for whom English is not their first language often did not hear explanations of what was being asked from them in terms they could understand.

---

and-get-the-shot-white-evangelical-leaders-push-covid-vaccine (accessed July 15, 2023); Brett Bachman, "MTG losing close to one-third of her Congressional salary to mask fines, spokesperson says," November 10, 2021, *Salon*, salon.com/2021/11/10/mtg-losing-close-to-one-third-of-her-congressional-salary-to-mask-fines-spokesperson-says/ (accessed July 15, 2023).

So what do we do? If such an egregious and immediate threat can no longer elicit a common response on the order of our national responses to Pearl Harbor or 9/11, where do we go from here? What we need is an ethic rooted deeply within America's dominant Abrahamic religious traditions but also philosophically compatible with the major streams of Asian religious thought. This ethic should also be acceptable to thoughtful people of no religious commitment whatsoever. No such idea will ever please or engage everyone. Nihilism, extreme capitalist greed, rank individualism, and other such approaches aren't interested in promoting the common good. The question then becomes, "Can we find a bedrock ethical principle that is both robust enough and flexible enough to allow Americans of good will to reach essential agreement on how we as a nation can best approach the challenges of the twenty-first century?" I believe we can.

As I have previously explained, my own tradition is that of an essentially orthodox, trinitarian Christian with a relatively high view of Scripture. As an adult, my intellectual journey has been to test that background against the demands and stresses of ongoing American social, scientific, and intellectual evolution. Increasing numbers of Americans have in recent years tested the ethical answers provided by traditional Christian thought and found them either wanting or, in some cases, misunderstood. The civil rights movement, for example, found its origin and much of its energy in challenging the racial status quo in the church. Both Black Americans and progressive white Christians found evidence in Scripture consistent with Jefferson's Lockian assertion in the Declaration of Independence that "all men [sic] are created equal." They took that essentially scriptural value, poorly supported in both Jefferson's personal life and in subsequent American political history, and made it a north star for the struggle and sacrifice that have advanced minority rights since the days of the Rev. Dr. Martin Luther King Jr. Basically, the assertion from the civil rights movement was that they understood and followed what Scripture was saying about human equality, while those who opposed them, even within the church, did not.

Attempting to tease out even a small percentage of the myriad crosscurrents and conflicts within contemporary Christianity alone would require a far longer book than I and an army of others could ever hope to write. Factoring in the ethical assertions and respective mythologies of Judaism, Islam, Hinduism, Buddhism, humanism, atheism, etc., would simply be impossible. Therefore, I will set forth what I believe to be the bedrock ethical principle for life contained within the Christian ideal of *agape* love and then attempt to argue that this single principle is both robust and flexible enough to serve a diverse society.

To begin, I want to tell you briefly about my friend and hero. This principle is expounded particularly in the writings of Baptist preacher, professor, and ethicist Henlee H. Barnette, who taught for more than a quarter century at The Southern Baptist Theological Seminary in Louisville, Kentucky, and wrote a number of short works addressing particular ethical issues as well as a textbook, *Introducing Christian Ethics*, that was used by at least two generations of college students and seminarians. Dr. Barnette was never widely recognized outside Baptist circles. His works were considered perhaps too pragmatic and too specifically biblically based, lacking the scholarly gravitas of his more academic and philosophically minded contemporaries. At the same time, formed in the tradition of his co-religionist hero Walter Rauschenbusch of social gospel fame, Barnette's studies resulted in a remarkable history of activism: helping found the first interracial Baptist pastors' conference in Birmingham, Alabama, in 1948; bringing Martin Luther King Jr. to speak at Southern

Seminary at the height of the civil rights era and almost getting himself fired in the process; and addressing across his long career a series of contemporary issues from racism to drugs to ecology.

In every case, when he approached a new issue, Barnette returned to what he called his core Christian tenet of "contextual, principled *agapism*." He defined *agape*, which is the Greek word used to describe God-like love, as essentially "to will and to work for the well-being of the other."[6] This is the primary word for Christian love used in the New Testament both by Jesus and by his apostles. Like Jesus himself, Barnette did not exclude maintaining the same kind of interest in one's own well-being, but his ethic was essentially other-directed, a way of approaching the world beyond one's own self.

Agape is just one of the Greek words for love. Along with *eros* and *phileo*, it describes a particular facet of the overall concept we refer to with the single English word "love." In the New Testament, Jesus and the apostles used *agape* when they were describing the kind of love God has for human beings and the kind of love humans are to aspire to in our concern for ourselves and one another. In effect, when Jesus says "God is love," this is what he means. It is not mere affection. Nor is it necessarily connected with emotions at all. As Barnette defines it, *agape* means to will and to work for the object of one's concern. Let's tease that out a bit.

First, love is an act of the will. It is not something that overwhelms us such as erotic passion. Nor is it something we fall into without conscious choice or decision on our part. It is something we do. We choose to work for the well-being of the one we love. On a broader scale, this means you and I need not necessarily approve of, like, or even want to be

---

6. Henlee Hulix Barnette, *Introducing Christian Ethics* (Nashville: Broadman, 1961), 59, 101–108.

around the object of our love. Instead, *agape* is a decision we make regardless of our personal affection for the object. We decide the individual, nation, class, or group is worthy of our good wishes and we choose to give them.

Second, love involves action. *Agape* is never merely benevolence. One can be positively disposed toward an individual, subgroup, or nation and wish them well. But you do not reach the level of *agape* love until you ask and answer the question, "What can I do about it?" Many of us, from all different perspectives, consider ourselves to be good, loving people because we do not harbor anger or ill will toward a particular group. One can say, "I love gay people!" or "I love immigrants!" or "I love right- (or left-)wingers!" Indeed, such statements are quite easy to make. But unless that love involves some sort of specific, concrete action for the benefit of the one loved, it is, in practice, meaningless.

Third, necessarily, *agape* takes a broader view of situations. When you and I think of the love of God, we tend to think of that love in terms of a more general, personally disinterested benevolence. When we think of our own loves, our focus tends to go more to the annoying neighbor or the arrogant boss or the maddening spouse or child. What *agape* asks, though, is that you and I discipline ourselves to look at every situation of life by attempting, at least, to ask how we can work for the well-being of the other *as they actually are*. As I write, for example, Israelis and Palestinians are once again at loggerheads. Blood has been shed. True *agape* applied in this situation would involve working to look toward both what could be done in the moment to defuse tensions and what could be done to move in the direction of long-term well-being for Palestinians and Israelis alike. Nobody ever said this would be easy. But this is the kind of simultaneous detachment and attention to which we must aspire.

Fourth, *agape*, in this sense, is willing to postpone the perfect in pursuit of the good. It acknowledges the gap between God's ideal and what you and I can presently achieve. In effect, it lives and works in the real world. When I wrote above of Barnette's approach, I called it, as he did, contextual, principled *agapism*. That means two things. It means *agape* as he conceived it is meaningless unless it operates within a specific context. It does no good to tell an impoverished child in Mississippi that you love them unless you are working to do the next thing that could help their individual life somehow be better. And then, secondly, principled *agapism* means that any movement toward real love will inevitably involve lesser, intermediate steps.

Justice, for example, is one of those steps. Justice is not love as such. But because justice entails treating people equitably and defending those who are being injured by others, justice is a principle of human behavior that moves in the direction of love. Similarly, honesty is such a principle. So is kindness. So is a commitment to scientific truth. The number of valid ethical principles entailed within *agape* is virtually limitless. A commitment to the dignity and self-determination of all persons comes to mind. So does respect for the earth. So does tolerance for the diversity of religions, cultures, and traditions.

In every case, the test for the validity of these various lesser principles is whether they support the goal of enhancing the well-being of the one being loved. That determination may not be easy. In the musical *Fiddler on the Roof*, faced by the challenges of being a faithful Jew in czarist Russia, the peasant Tevye often argues with himself by carrying out an internal dialogue. "One the one hand," he says, then, "On the other hand." His methodology reaches its limit when he has to decide whether to bless his daughter's love for a Christian man. In perhaps the musical's most memorable line, he realizes he cannot stretch his tolerance so far and proclaims, "There is no other hand!" He simply cannot believe loving his daughter could mean approving of her union with one outside his faith. His sectarian intransigence in that moment stands as an example of what may be the greatest ongoing challenge to our twenty-first-century society's development of an ethic of *agape* according to our putative definition. Closed-mindedness often cannot imagine well-being beyond certain limited and specific boundaries. Eventually Tevye's position softens, but only after a great deal of struggle, heartache, and alienation.

In essence, then, fifth, well-being must necessarily be an evolving concept. Any attempt to define well-being rigidly, universally, and permanently is limited by the reality of human development. In this present world, we simply do not and cannot know everything that is and needs to be known. There's a little noticed but fascinating saying of Jesus in his final discourse to the disciples in the Gospel of John. Talking with them about the Holy Spirit, which is to be the presence of God with them after Jesus is gone, he says in John 16:12-13, "I still have many things to say to you, but you cannot bear them now. When the Spirit of truth comes, he will guide you into all the truth" (NRSV). In other words, contrary to all fundamentalist orthodoxy, Jesus never said either the Scripture or his own words were to be the end of human learning. Instead, he said precisely the opposite.

In this sense, genuine Christian orthodoxy is always in harmony with, and absolutely not antithetical to, the secular scientific concept of a constant, never-ending search for knowledge. Instead of limiting human understanding and action to a particular place, time, and incarnation of society as various Christian churches, sects, and preachers have done throughout two millennia of history, the founder of this religion opens the door to an ongoing human journey of growth and learning.

Note, though, that this journey of human growth from an authentically Christian perspective is emphatically not without guidance and standards. That guidance is entailed within the concept of *agape* love itself. To want and to work for the well-being of ourselves, others, and all creation is *the* Christian journey. Anything less is necessarily inadequate.

The challenge, sixth, is to identify and pursue the most loving course of action in the given situation in which we find ourselves. Over half a century ago, Joseph Fletcher attempted to thread the needle between moral absolutism and moral relativism.[7] His argument, which was promptly vilified both from the right and the left, was that pursuit of the loving thing in any situation would lead to the best available moral decision in that situation. In effect, Fletcher was arguing that legalism did not permit sufficient flexibility to address the vast array of moral questions presented by modern life. He thought paring absolutes down to the single principle of love would provide all the guidance needed.

Barnette, who debated Fletcher in person on one occasion, argued that the lack in Fletcher's theory was its failure to provide adequate principled content for the nature of love as guidance in decision-making. For him the danger was that Fletcher's concept was so loose as to lend itself to the rampant antinomianism (i.e., a lack of rules in society) that many conservatives view as the primary danger in contemporary culture. With Barnette, I would argue that *agape* as we have defined it is robust and specific enough as well as flexible enough to provide the common anchor twenty-first-century society requires in order to move forward together.

---

7. *Situation Ethics: The New Morality* (Louisville: Westminster John Knox, 1966).

It does not leave us prey to antinomianism. Nor does it leave us without guidance. And it provides room for growth in human knowledge to allow us to expand our moral umbrella beyond outmoded prejudices and legalisms. It impels us toward a positive and healthy ethic for human progress. The challenge we face is learning how to practice such an ethic consistently and well.

As I write, we are faced with multiple examples of the difficulties inherent in practicing such an ethic. Vivid in many Americans' minds in early fall 2021 is the recent spectacle of the precipitate collapse of the Kabul government in Afghanistan as Americans finally withdrew combat troops from Afghanistan after twenty years. In a matter of days, the government's three hundred thousand troops simply laid down their arms and abandoned their posts in the face of the Taliban resurgence. At the same time, civilian governments in city after city collapsed. The American sphere of influence shrank virtually overnight to the Kabul airport and its environs as the US sought to evacuate our citizens and allies without new combat engagements with the Taliban. Condemnations of the lack of American intelligence about the Kabul government's complete corruption and of President Biden's withdrawal strategy were quick and vicious.

The President repeatedly declared that it was time for the Americans to leave and the Afghans to take charge of their own destiny. Critics argued that we should not have abandoned our Afghan friends to their fate and that some sort of American military presence should have been maintained. No alternative seemed to be without serious ongoing consequences.

At the same time, a second example of the difficulties inherent in ethical practice was unfolding in the continuing debate over national policies related to America's battle with Covid-19. Many Americans and national corporations cheered the President's announcement that federal employees and all employees of corporations with more than 100 employees as well as all that did business with the federal government must be vaccinated. This was seen as exactly the right thing to do in the face of a public health emergency reminiscent of the polio epidemic of the 1950s, still vivid in the memories of older Americans.

On the other side of the question, almost a third of the nation's adults continued to resist getting the vaccine or allowing children to be vaccinated, arguing that the government mandates were an unacceptable abuse of an individual's freedom to choose for themselves regarding their personal health and the health of their children. Legal conservatives argued that the Biden administration's use of existing OSHA regulations to justify the corporate mandate went beyond the scope intended when the law was written. In late fall, litigation on this matter reached the US Supreme Court. The court, as often happens, split the difference, upholding the mandate for healthcare institutions accepting federal funds but striking it down for large corporations.

Yet a third example emerged in summer 2021 as the Texas state legislature passed a novel anti-abortion law, banning all abortions after the detection of a fetal heartbeat (usually about six weeks after conception) and empowering individual citizens to sue individuals and medical providers who failed to abide by that standard. In this case, many of the same people and groups who were arguing against vaccine mandates as an attack on individual freedoms sought essentially to overturn *Roe v. Wade* by creating citizen vigilantes with the assignment of punishing women and doctors who exercised a woman's right to control her own body. A second law passed in Mississippi prohibited abortions after fifteen weeks past conception, about two months earlier than had been general practice under *Roe v. Wade*.

This latter debate was in no way new. It simply revived the more than half-century-old debate in the US over when human life begins and when a fetus becomes a person separate from its mother and deserving independent protection by the state. To put the question in graphic ethical terms, how can we as a society will and work for the well-being of a woman and her fetus at the same time? At what point should we even make the attempt?

A fourth example of an issue where people of good intentions differ on their approach to right and wrong has emerged in the continuing conversations regarding climate change. As we will discuss in chapter 6, this debate harks back to the worldview that often divides evangelical Christians from the larger Christian world. Evangelicals tend to focus on a particular eschatological reading of the Scriptures that sees this present world as already passing away as we move toward the climax of history with the second coming to earth of Jesus Christ. Traditional and progressive Christians also believe that Christ will come again, but they tend to leave how and when that happens to Christ himself and to focus their attention more on living faithfully in this present world.

A fifth such example emerges in the continuing American conversation over the nature and practice of human sexuality. While the biological and psychological realities of gay sexual orientation have been accepted by a majority of the scientific community and broad swaths of the public, and while gay marriage is now required to be recognized in every state, significant groups of conservative Christians continue to view any practice of same-gender sexuality as sinful and abhorrent to God. In 2022, the immediate conversation has largely shifted to the subject of transgender people as conservative state legislatures have worked to block gender-affirming health care for minors diagnosed with gender dysphoria. In

addition, the Supreme Court decision that denied a constitutional right to abortion has also reopened the question
of whether the implied right to privacy in the Fourteenth
Amendment protects the right to gay marriage. In many
ways, this latter conversation continues symbolically the
unresolved debate within Christian circles over the precise
nature of biological creation and the degree to which the
church can or should support the individual journeys of
those who seek to pursue gender or sexual identity outside
traditional heterosexual, cisgender norms.

Finally, it's difficult to compile any list of ethical challenges in American life in the first quarter of the twenty-first
century without coming face to face with the issue of gun
control. Perhaps nothing is as painful for us as the continuing
agony of how to keep one another—and especially our children—safe from gun violence.

In the following chapters, I will attempt to unpack some
of the strategies I believe we as a society should seek to use
to inform our ongoing conversations. We'll look at how we
proceed to have difficult conversations, to make and act on
difficult decisions, and to remain open to change as new facts
and new understandings come to light. In each chapter, I'll
return to one of the six issues I've identified above and seek
to explore it more fully, asking how *agape* and its subsidiary
values can inform both Christian conversation and specific
attitudes and actions moving forward. Most of all, I hope to
suggest ways in which we can strengthen the motto that still
graces our currency and with which we began as a nation. *E
Pluribus Unum.* Out of many, one.

Questions for Reflection and Discussion

1. Describe your view of the place of the Bible as a guide for contemporary living. Do you see it as a rule book? A general but nonspecific guide? Limited to the Ten Commandments? Irrelevant to modern life? A set of ideals? Something else? Write down your answer in your own words and refer back to it as we go through the remainder of this book.

2. This book makes a great deal of Jesus's commandment to his followers to practice *agape*, love defined as "to will and to work for the well-being of others and oneself." Note that this definition does not include our normal cultural definition of love as an intense feeling. How would you go about separating these two concepts in working toward an ethical decision?

3. The author lists several divisive issues that helped prompt the writing of this book. The list is by no means exhaustive. What current ethical issues would you like this book to help you find a way to work through?

4. If you are part of a different religious tradition from the author, are there bedrock principles in your tradition that you use to help you make decisions on issues? How do you go about that process?.

Chapter 3

Right and Wrong in American Foreign Policy

In chapter 2 I first raised the issue of the US exit from Afghanistan in late summer 2021 as an example of conflicting opinions in Christian ethics. Conversation over the rightness or wrongness of that exit has continued since it took place.

Some have taken a kind of *Realpolitik* view that the exit was inevitable. History has shown repeatedly that powers foreign to Afghanistan fail to possess either the understanding or the will to succeed in transforming the tumultuous environment in that country. We could dominate it militarily for a season, as long as we were willing to invest the blood and treasure to do so. But we could not change either the values or perceptions of the Afghan people. In this view, our experiment in building a Western-style democracy there was doomed sooner or later to fail. Spending more money, more time, or more lives there would be an exercise in futility. This attitude, among other things, tapped into profound public weariness with America's longest war and deepening public resentment at the continuing loss of American lives in Afghanistan.

Others, both from the right and the left of the American political spectrum, have argued that our exit betrayed both our Afghan partners and our own best values. The political left points to the immediate losses suffered by Afghan women as the Americans exited. Schools for girls were shuttered. Women were required to return to traditional dress. Most tellingly, the new Taliban government was overwhelmingly and unapologetically male. University and business access for women was swiftly restricted. In addition, those women and men who had worked for or with the American forces and had been promised that the US would never abandon them quickly discovered that "never" wasn't nearly as far away as they had thought. Despite heroic evacuation efforts by the US military, many translators and others found themselves unable to secure visas to enter the US. Those outside the immediate vicinity of the Kabul airport found it nearly impossible to leave Afghanistan.

By the same token, the right, with the substantial agreement of America's military leadership, continued to argue that they could succeed in transforming and pacifying Afghanistan if they were given the money, the troops, and enough time to do so. This less than subtle disagreement with administration policy contributed substantially to a first-year impression on the part of many that President Biden was proving to be a weak and ineffective leader. Many Americans continue to believe that America both can and should do anything and everything possible to enhance and expand democracy and political freedom around the world. This belief on the part of many Christians was also linked to a pious view that any nation we could ultimately open to Christian conversion, whether we said that was what we were doing or not, would ultimately be better off.

Before we can apply any of the ethical yardsticks I have suggested to this kind of geopolitical situation, though, we must first at least briefly deal with the question of whether it is appropriate to apply Christian ethical standards to politics at all. Certainly, it is not easy. Reinhold Niebuhr, in his classic twentieth-century work *Moral Man and Immoral Society*, argued that a distinction must always be made between individual and corporate ethics. At the same time, he came to believe, particularly with reference to the Nazi menace, that Christians must be ready to oppose evil by whatever means are necessary including violence. In this sense, Niebuhrian ethics argues that at times Christians must be content with less than perfect standards such as justice in order to approximate Christian goals in an imperfect world.

For example, as we have said, the highest ethical standard for Christians is *agape*, love defined as willing and working for the well-being of the one loved. To attempt to apply that standard in a situation such as the invasion of Afghanistan, you must first define the object of your intentions. Were we there to express *agape* toward Osama bin Laden and the forces of Al Qaeda? The people of Afghanistan? The people of the United States? The military? Christians are often fond of saying they love everybody. That may well be true in the abstract. But when you encounter a complex geopolitical situation involving Islamic terrorists, innocent civilians, a completely foreign history and culture, the dynamics of military intervention, and the often fickle and shifting political demands of American voters, you can quickly see that working for the well-being of some necessarily involves working against the interests of others.

A lesser standard such as justice becomes the only realistic Judeo-Christian yardstick that can be applied. We went to Afghanistan in the first instance because that was where Osama bin Laden and his lieutenants chose to hide and to use as their base of operations. That mission quickly expanded to include taking down the Taliban regime and attempting to rebuild Afghan military and civilian life on a more democratic model as a hedge against future radical terrorism. By the time bin Laden had clearly left Afghanistan and gone to ground elsewhere, the initial mission to get him and the rest of the Al Qaeda leadership had morphed into an attempt to remake Afghan society after Western standards. Politically, militarily, educationally, and societally, American military and diplomatic efforts were, in effect, working to reshape an essentially medieval Islamic culture by twenty-first-century American standards.

Much of what we attempted was admirable, even noble, and, while by no means specifically Christian, essentially in harmony with Christian values. Efforts to expand medical care and educational opportunities in the countryside, especially for women and girls, enabled an entire generation of Afghan women to hope for a better life in ways they had never been able to do before. Supporting efforts to allow for democratic government worked to replace traditional tribal power structures and to allow for more genuine self-determination by the Afghan people. In an attempt to provide security for these efforts, the US and our allies poured billions of dollars into building the Afghan army and assigned military advisers to spend years working to shape 300,000 Afghans into a competent fighting force.

Over two decades of effort there, thousands of American military, civilian, and governmental workers made many friends for the US. Significant numbers of Afghans caught a vision for a different way of life. At the same time, American efforts suffered from an essential, ultimately fatal naivete. We thought twenty years of investment in the Afghan people and government would be sufficient to counterbalance a millennium of Indigenous culture.

Before the end of the first Christian millennium, church thinkers began to realize that the standards of individual piety Jesus left us in his teachings could not be translated without interpretation into geopolitical issues. They began to develop what became known as the Just War theory. In effect, it taught that Christians could support a war if the conduct of the war itself met a series of ethical standards. The list of those standards has changed a good deal through history, but perhaps the most practical and enduring of those is the test of proportionality. It suggests that Christians can consider a war just if the cost of that war in lives, suffering, and treasure is less than the attainable benefit to be derived.

With regard to Afghanistan, what became clear to many American leaders over the two decades we spent in Afghanistan was that changes required in Afghan polity and culture to attain a stable democratic society were so difficult to achieve that it was impossible to anticipate an end in any kind of time frame the American people would be willing to support. The end, a free and stable Afghanistan, while it was much to be desired, was not proportional to the blood, treasure, and time it would have taken to achieve that end. Ultimately President Biden and his advisers decided that it was time for America to leave direct combat there and to seek change in that society by much longer-term diplomatic means. Public opinion on leaving was divided. At this writing, it remains to be seen whether Biden and his political party will pay a price at the polls for his decision. (As it turned out, not much!) Yet the rule of proportionality suggests that in this instance the American decision to withdraw met the test of justice.

The manner of the withdrawal is another matter. As part of leaving, the US promised those Afghans who had served as interpreters, advisers, or in other supportive positions for American troops that they would receive accelerated consideration for immigration visas to the United States if they wished to leave Afghanistan. For many of these people, leaving the country as the Taliban took over became a matter of life and death. True justice in this situation would include justice for these people and their families.

A similar dilemma is unfolding in the Ukraine as I write. The villain in this case is Russia's Vladimir Putin, though Americans such as former President Trump have expressed admiration and support for Putin's invasion of his immediate neighbor even as the attack on an independent and sovereign nation goes forward.

It's impossible to understand America's willingness to support Ukraine's nascent democracy financially and with substantial military resources excluding combat troops without a lesson in European history. The short version is that, even though NATO has admitted the Baltic republics, which also directly border Russia, Ukraine's turn to the West has developed more gradually and perhaps more tentatively than these other former Soviet republics. As the largest and richest of the former Soviet republics in Europe, Ukraine is also seen by Russians to be more essential to their own nation's well-being. Its seeking membership in NATO, even though NATO and the US have said clearly that Ukraine is nowhere near ready for such membership, so alarmed President Putin, and so aggravated his hatred of NATO, that Putin sees subduing Ukraine as essential to Russian well-being and its standing as a "great power" in the Soviet tradition.

The problem the United States has is twofold. First, as a next-door neighbor, Ukraine's interest in moving toward the West could legitimately be seen as a concern for Russia. Second, Russia retains a standing army and a nuclear arsenal second only to that of the United States itself. Direct American involvement in combat in Ukraine would risk nothing short of a nuclear conflagration. Putin has threatened no less.

Biden's dilemma is how to support the freedom-loving people of the Ukraine without provoking a much wider and more devastating war in Europe and beyond. As in Afghanistan, there is a profound gap in Ukraine between a Christian ideal of secure peace and freedom for the Ukrainians and what could likely be achieved without devastating consequences for Europe and the world at large. And yet, as the war in Ukraine has continued, several realities are becoming progressively clearer.

First, Ukraine differs significantly from Afghanistan in that its people have chosen to turn their interest and allegiance toward the West. And they have been willing to fight and die to protect their national sovereignty in a way that the Afghanis as a whole never were.

Second, Putin's brutal invasion of Ukraine has alarmed western Europe to such a degree that the NATO alliance has become more unified in purpose and intentions than at almost any point since the end of World War II. NATO's welcome of previously neutral Finland and Sweden into the alliance and its commitment to beef up its own military resources suggests that, rather than be cowed by what Russia has done in Ukraine, NATO has been emboldened.

Third, Ukraine's warm reception by the European Union, along with growing financial and military support from the West, suggest that Europe is likely to continue to do whatever is necessary to ensure that Ukraine is able to maintain its sovereignty in the face of Russian aggression. To fail to do so would be to capitulate to Russian expansionism, and that capitulation seems less and less likely. Exactly what Ukrainian sovereignty will look like in the years ahead does not yet emerge.

Fourth, as the war continues into its second year, both the international response to Russia's ongoing brutality toward the Ukrainians and its enormous waste of its own blood and treasure in a war in which it seems unlikely to achieve its objectives in any timely or ultimately satisfactory fashion suggest that it is increasingly likely to fail. Christian just war theory suggests that a war that cannot be won without unreasonable pain and suffering for the antagonists should never be fought in the first place and should be ended as expeditiously as possible.

All this means that the efforts of the United States and the NATO allies to provide Ukraine with the money and materiel needed to defend itself can be considered from a just war standpoint to be money well spent. It may not win the war, but in this case American involvement remains worth its cost.

I began my practical examinations of the ways a Christian ethic of right and wrong grounded in *agape* can apply today with these examples of situations in which that ethic is severely limited as a cautionary tale. Many Christians continue to view the application of biblical standards to contemporary life as direct and easy. Sometimes it is. You do not steal your neighbor's car or your neighbor's spouse. But even then one could imagine exceptions that might be justified. Taking a car without permission to get someone quickly to the hospital might be justified. Helping an abused spouse to escape from that abuse could be the only Christian thing to do. In the chapters to come, we will look at other issues Americans face in the twenty-first century. In each case we will look at ways in which an ethic grounded in *agape* can inform American thinking as we move forward. Deciding whether the approach I suggest is adequate to the task is up to the reader. My hope is that, at the very least, this exercise will encourage serious thinking about what it means to be an intelligent Christian in this present world.

Questions for Reflection and Discussion

1. Do you have a personal or family background in business, military, or governmental foreign service? If so, or if not, how does your own experience affect your attitude toward American involvement abroad?

2. Afghanistan is often described as "America's longest war." Despite nearly twenty years' involvement, the loss of numerous American lives, and the expenditure of billions of dollars, we did not succeed creating a democratic society there. Why not? Was it time to conclude our efforts? Just War Theory suggests that for a war to have been begun in Afghanistan, it should have been possible to win with a reasonable or "proportionate" expenditure of blood and treasure by the United States. We should have been able to achieve our objective without too much pain. Or do you believe it was inherently just Or was it inherently just?

3. In Ukraine, America is expending billions in military and economic aid without the direct involvement of American troops. Do you see this as a more or less "just" way for American involvement than we practiced in Afghanistan?

4. In this issue, the principle of *agape* is applied only through the lesser principle of seeking justice for the people of Ukraine. This "real world" application of justice as a principle of action for Christians has a long history dating back to the Middle Ages. Is violence always a necessary option for the interactions of governments?

Chapter 4

America Questions What's Right in a Pandemic

In January 2020, my family and I escaped winter in Colorado to spend a couple of weeks in California, celebrating our son's birthday and meeting friends for sightseeing in and around San Diego. We had begun to hear rumblings about the emergence of a new strain of virus erupting in Wuhan in China. It was rumored to be highly contagious and potentially dangerous since no one had any kind of immunity to this previously unseen disease. We had seen novel viruses erupt before with varying degrees of severity. I remember offering to snap a photo of a group of Chinese tourists walking along a seaside park in La Jolla. I took the camera with no concern and took the picture of the grateful family with hardly a second thought. I do remember joking with my family later that I hoped they weren't from Wuhan. But that was about the last moment of levity regarding the virus for at least the next two years.

Quickly dubbed Covid-19, by the middle of March the virus had been declared a pandemic. Government, medical institutions, and pharmaceutical companies around the world found themselves facing illnesses and deaths unseen in the general population since the flu pandemic of 1918–1920. On the advice of the Center for Disease Control, my wife and I, as senior adults, and I as a Type 1 diabetic, stopped attending church, arranged curbside pickup of our groceries, curtailed face-to-face contact with friends and family, and, in short, entered the longest period of isolation in our lives.

In the meantime, the pharmaceutical industry began a race to develop a Covid vaccine in record time. Vaccine development had traditionally been a long, tedious trial-and-error process. It could take years, or even decades, from the time vaccine research for a particular disease was begun until a suitable formula was found, tested in human trials with volunteers, and approved by the government for use with the public. I well remember as a school-aged child in the 1950s receiving the polio vaccine on a sugar cube at school. Physicians and parents at that time were massively relieved to finally have an effective weapon against a disease that struck without warning and often resulted in paralysis or death. I was too young to have been privy to any conversations questioning the vaccine's safety. But just like smallpox, measles, mumps, and tetanus shots, polio vaccination quickly became a required step to take for any child entering public school.

With Covid, though, the development process evolved far more quickly than with any previous vaccine. Two companies led the way in America. Pfizer and Moderna were both ready to request FDA and CDC approval for Emergency Use Authorization for their vaccines by early autumn 2020. The requests at this stage were limited to those who were either sixteen or eighteen years old and over. By early December, the first company was granted its EUA, and beginning with medical personnel and the most vulnerable, shots began to be distributed at near breakneck speed.

And there began the problems. Few people questioned the priorities established for who could access the vaccinations when and in what order. Quickly, though, a backlash began to develop among right-wing media, especially among white male conservatives, who questioned the efficacy, safety, and necessity of the vaccines for otherwise healthy adults. Both the Pfizer and the Moderna vaccines used a novel technology manipulating MRNA molecules in the virus to produce shots that extensive clinical trials showed to be more than 90 percent effective in preventing hospitalization and death from Covid, an almost unheard-of degree of efficacy. The success of the venture, though, seemed to feed deep suspicion among significant segments of the public.

In the medical community, despite frequent assurances from FDA and CDC officials and the White House task force charged with distributing the vaccines and promoting them to the public, and despite growing pressure to require the vaccines for medical, and especially hospital, personnel, significant minorities began to assert their individual rights and refuse all pressure to comply. That refusal to comply has continued to be asserted as an individual right by first responders, workers in vital industries, and even members of the military throughout the pandemic. In spring 2022, the Air Force Academy here in Colorado withheld commissions from three members of the graduating class because, despite orders, they continued to refuse to be vaccinated.

At the same time the first vaccines were being submitted for emergency authorization, the 2020 presidential election took place. The vast majority of Democrats strongly supported efforts by the FDA, the CDC, and the medical community at large to convince Americans to take the vaccine as soon as they became eligible. While the Trump White House had done significant work both to encourage the development of vaccines and to secure large supplies of the vaccines for public use as soon as they were approved, the question of requiring vaccines for workers in essential industries such as medicine, food supply, and defense and especially the issue of whether masking should be required in public spaces as a safety measure soon became a political football with the incoming Biden Administration pushing hard for such measures and the outgoing Trump Administration attempting both to take credit for the vaccines and to emphasize individual freedoms over public health. President Trump himself was notoriously resistant to wearing a mask, even with his own advisers busily encouraging everyone else to do so.

Throughout the pandemic, the Biden White House has been unequivocal in encouraging and, when it could do so, requiring as many Americans as possible to take both the vaccines and the boosters when they subsequently came on the scene. Far fewer Republicans both at the federal and the state levels have supported campaigns for vaccination—and many have actively resisted all such efforts. Evangelical Christians have been particularly reluctant to comply with public health orders regarding gathering for worship. Many evangelicals have gone even further and taken refuge in an essentially superstitious approach to the whole issue, claiming, "I don't need the vaccine. Jesus will protect me!"

All of this raises the question of what Christian attitudes and responses should be in the midst of a public health crisis such as the Covid-19 pandemic. Should Christians simply leave decisions about such matters up to individuals, and/ or can we affirm a difference between what is right in such a situation for Christians and what is wrong?

We can dismiss the "Jesus will protect me!" argument without much investigation. It amounts to superstition rather than faith and completely ignores the reality that Jesus never promised to protect Christians from the normal vicissitudes of human life such as disability, aging, and disease. Instead, we are given the tools of intelligence, science, and curiosity to enable us to work with the Holy Spirit to improve and protect human life.

If we go back, however, to our initial assertion that Jesus calls us to live according to *agape* both toward ourselves and toward those we love personally as well as the larger community, we find a number of ways in which thoughtful Christian ethics does speak to events such as the Covid pandemic and our response to it.

First and foremost, to will and to work for the well-being of the human community means that Christians should support immediate and coordinated efforts to address such an emergency as soon as it arises. For many Americans, that assertion runs directly counter to their own allegiance to the American mythology of rugged individualism and absolute individual autonomy. The truth, though, is that mythology has never been without qualification in the face of emergencies. We as Americans are justifiably proud of our governmental emergency services and our strong heritage of volunteerism. When there's a problem, we tend to show up and do whatever we can to help.

It's in precisely that spirit that first responders, medical personnel, researchers, politicians, and even the pharmaceutical industry immediately focused their energies on understanding and protecting us all from Covid-19 as soon as we began to realize there was a problem. These initial responses were tentative and incomplete. The information available to the public changed daily and weekly in the early months of the pandemic as we sought to understand the nature of the virus, how it is transmitted, and the best interim measures for minimizing the spread of infection while we waited for researchers to develop and test potential treatments and vaccines. The process was messy and frustrating. Its perhaps most unfortunate side effect was to aggravate the already rampant American suspicion of experts and of governmental authority. Unfortunately, that messiness played into the longstanding debate in American society between those who advocate for and support government efforts to improve social conditions for society as a whole and those who believe individual freedom should trump government involvement in individual lives whenever possible.

Objections to vaccination requirements for employment or travel seem to boil down largely to a conflict between individual rights and the responsibility of government to act for the common good. For example, if I consider my individual right to make my own healthcare decisions without regard to the well-being of others, it becomes easy to say I don't think I need or want a particular vaccine. In the early days of the pandemic, I often encountered people who both claimed to be devout Christians and maintained that they had every right to work with or fly on an airplane alongside others while choosing not to be vaccinated or wear a mask or take any of the other elementary precautions recommended by infectious disease professionals. This was happening at the same time that people were sickening and dying at increasingly alarming rates throughout the United States.

Other than the "Jesus will protect me" argument, which is mere superstition, and various conspiracy theories concocted by the political far right (e.g., the vaccines contain mind-control computer chips), individual autonomy seemed to be the only argument offered. The problem here is that nothing in Scripture as a whole or the teachings of Jesus in particular comes remotely close to validating a doctrine of absolute individual autonomy. Instead, Jesus's command to love God with all our heart and soul and mind and strength and to love others as we love ourselves requires a Christian way of being that takes the utmost care to consider the welfare of others in every decision we make and every act we take concerning our existence in community.

It should go without saying, though no commonsense assumption seems to go without saying in contemporary America, that the first part of good decision-making in a novel emergency such as the Covid-19 pandemic is to listen to the counsel of medical experts as it emerges. Clearly, when faced with a societal challenge such as the pandemic presented, Christians should be the first to take recommended preventive measures such as wearing masks and social distancing. And we should have been among the earliest to seek to access vaccines as they became available to the various age groups and medical conditions within the population. Only by taking those measures could we hope to care for ourselves and others as Covid continued to evolve and spread throughout society. That would be the right thing to do.

Astonishingly, though, significant segments of the Christian community, led by many clergy, seemed to place lesser values above working toward the well-being of the community. It's no accident, for example, that one of the first places where a widespread infection occurred was in a large church choir in the Pacific northwest. In that one outbreak, more than forty people were infected and several died. In fairness, that outbreak occurred early on, before even the experts were certain that the virus is transmitted largely through respiration. What is surprising is the Christian community's reluctance to learn from that early event and others.

Because people in worship services are typically close together, because Christian worship includes choral and congregational singing as a significant feature in virtually every service, and because the virus is spread through respi- ration, as soon as that fact was known churches should have been among the first places to institute safety precautions such as masking and social distancing. Many refused. Many pastors in various parts of the country saw the recommended safety measures as somehow an attack on Christianity. Instead of leading their congregations to support medical and governmental efforts to encourage safety measures and support vaccination efforts, some pastors chose to hold crowded worship services even in defiance of public health orders in the worst days of the pandemic. As a consequence, many died and the reputation of the church suffered signif- icant erosion in public respect. Refusal by churches to implement expert advice as it became available proved both self-defeating and, I would argue, objectively wrong in terms of Christian teaching.

It would also be wrong to suggest that all American churches were cavalier with safety concerns during the pandemic. Many congregations limited the size of congre- gational meetings, instituted social distancing in worship, or even suspended in-person worship in favor of broadcasting services online. That interruption in normal procedures didn't end in many congregations until vaccines became generally available. Older and immunocompromised communicants, particularly, continued to worship online or to mask for worship even as others relaxed precautions. And many faith communities were instrumental in encouraging people to be vaccinated and tested and to observe isolation protocols if they became infected.

Subvariants of the virus continue to make their way through area after area of the country. So far there have been at least four national peaks in infections, hospitalizations, and deaths. As of May 2023, 1.1 million Americans, most of them over age sixty-five, have died, far more than documented in any other nation. At the same time, those who wish to be vaccinated and boosted have been able to access at least four successive shots, and public health authorities continue to keep people informed when infections and hospitalizations rise in their local areas. All Americans over six months old are now eligible to be vaccinated. By far the great majority of those who have died have been the unvaccinated.

At present, most Americans have either been vaccinated and boosted and observe precautions when counseled to do so, or they have chosen not to do so and continue to assume that personal risk for themselves. We are moving from a pandemic stage of the virus in the United States to what is likely to be an endemic one. The virus will most likely continue to be with us for the foreseeable future. From an ethical standpoint, the question I'd like to end this chapter with is, "What should American Christians do with regard to Covid-19 from here forward?"

I contend that living by *agape* as Jesus commanded means Christians are called to work for the well-being of our local, national, and international communities whether it happens to be convenient for us as individuals or not. "Jesus will protect me" is, at bottom, a profoundly selfish and short-sighted way to live in addition to being heresy. Similarly, the idea that "I have the right to make my own decisions regardless of risk to others!" is antithetical to Christ's call to be concerned for others in all that we do.

Questions for Discussion and Reflection

1. The pandemic is still a very real and raw experience for many people. It's important as you attempt any discussion to devote some time to reflect on people's experiences. Chances are feelings may be quite strong about what was and was not done to meet the challenges the virus produced.

2. Much of the discussion around responses to the pandemic had to do with the incomplete and evolving nature of the scientific and medical responses to the virus. How should people of good will respond in the middle of such a rapidly changing situation?

3. What is the appropriate role of political leadership in an emergency such as the pandemic? In 2020 and 2021, responses to events related to the pandemic became highly politicized. How should politicians and scientists work together regarding matters of public health?

4. Does an individual have an ethical right to refuse vaccination for a contagious disease if that refusal may cause them to infect others with whom they associate? For example, does a teacher or health worker have a personal right to refuse vaccination when they are in daily contact with at-risk people?

Chapter 5

Americans Search for Right and Wrong Regarding Abortion

The ongoing debate about whether the abortion of a fetus is right or wrong has captured the attention of segments of American Christianity for more than half a century now. From the time when the US Supreme Court in its 1973 *Roe v. Wade* decision found that a woman's right to privacy included the right to abortion to summer 2022 when a philosophically different Court found that there is no such constitutional right, the battle has raged. Untold amounts of time, energy, money, and debate have failed to resolve what a definitive Christian position on abortion ought to be. I frankly doubt that this chapter will solve that problem either, but it does serve as an interesting test of the limits of the ethical standard I am supporting.

The Roman Catholic Church continues to be a major actor in this ongoing drama. Catholic doctrine has long held that human life begins at conception and that there is no excuse sufficient to terminate a pregnancy before its natural result, whatever that result might be. Some extremely conservative Protestants, claiming frequent abuses of *Roe v. Wade* by those using abortion as "a form of birth control," choose also to argue that "life is life." The fetus, they argue, always deserves as much protection as the mother from those who would interrupt its development.

By the mid-twentieth century, many mainline Protestant traditions and even some more conservative communions had allowed that pregnancy might legitimately be terminated under conditions such as conception by rape or incest, significant fetal defect, or when necessary to protect the life of the mother. Even Southern Baptist Convention resolutions in the 1960s supported this kind of flexible standard. More liberal communions went so far as to suggest that abortion was a private matter between a woman, her family, and her physician. This kind of flexibility was also in line with long-standing Jewish tradition that made fetal life clearly secondary to the life of the mother and saw any decision to terminate a pregnancy as a private matter.

Interestingly enough, a feature article in the online edition of the *New York Times*, July 14, 2022, contains interviews with Americans who identify as pro-life and a second sample of people identifying as pro-choice and found that things aren't so simple. There are circumstances under which many pro-life people would accept abortion as appropriate and necessary, and there are circumstances in which many pro-choice people would be reluctant or opposed to the termination of a pregnancy.

The question here is "Can Jesus's teaching of *agape*, love defined as the effort to will and to work for the well-being of all concerned, bring us to clarity in how Christian individuals should support and/or oppose the mother's right to choose to terminate a pregnancy?" I believe it can.

In order to move toward clarity, though, we must first define the terms of the conversation. This definition is my own, and I must bear responsibility both before God and as a lifelong Christian minister for the things I am about to write. In so doing I am attempting to take seriously scriptural guidance, Christian tradition, and my own experience of the personhood of Jesus. No matter what I say, some will be certain that I've gotten it wrong. So be it.

First, in my mind, we start with the nature and actions of God. "Then the LORD God formed man from the dust of the ground and breathed into his nostrils the breath of life, and the man became a living being" (Gen 2:7, NRSV). Right away, we run headlong into the problem of biblical interpretation. From this particular text, I take two specific affirmations. God is involved in the creation of human life and has been so from the beginning of creation. And something significant happens at birth, or perhaps at viability, that affirms the status of the fetus as "alive" and worthy of protection as an individual. This second affirmation is debatable. I believe, however, that the Scripture suggests the fetus before viability remains "potential" human life and should be under the care of the prospective parents and their medical advisers.

Second, though, we must examine the responsibility of the parents, both prospective mother and father, with regard to fetal care. Ideally, in the twenty-first century no child should be born who is not wanted and planned for. In Christian thinking, sexually active adults have a moral responsibility to make certain that their efforts at procreation take place within the context of ample provision and nurture.

At the most basic level, this means Christian couples who are unwilling or unable to contemplate a pregnancy with joy have a prima facie responsibility to practice contraception in their sex life. This assertion runs counter to Roman Catholic teaching though not to the practice of a large percentage of Catholic laity in their childbearing years. Similarly, Protestants assume that planning their procreation so as to limit the number of their children to those they can both care for and receive with joy is part of the responsibility of married life. Simply put, for Christians, the question of an "unwanted pregnancy" should not arise. Jewish teaching also assumes the right and responsibility of prospective parents to make their own decisions about whether to bring a child into the world or not. And secular Americans have long assumed that the right of making their own reproductive choices is part of responsible adulthood.

While fetal life must therefore be highly valued and treated with care, this does not mean that fetal life necessarily must be assigned independent value as an individual apart from its parents, especially in the early stages of pregnancy. For example, there is no specific biblical tradition regarding in vitro fertilization and implantation of embryos because such a thing simply did not exist in biblical times. It is an innovation of modern medicine designed to give couples who otherwise would not be able to become parents the ability to do so. Because conception even in a laboratory is not an exact science, the process at current states of technology may necessarily involve the creation of embryos that are not subsequently implanted for gestation.

In addition the birth mother and father at all stages of gestation have a responsibility to see that the fetus receives optimal care. For the male parent, this care necessarily operates at one remove. The fetus is not nurtured in the male body (transgender pregnancy excepted). That means while the male can and should be supportive, the female necessarily retains ultimate responsibility along with her physician for determining whether a specific pregnancy should continue to term or not.

With the above assertion, we once again find ourselves returning to the standard of *agape* love set by Jesus. The responsibility of the prospective parents and of their physician is to will and work for the well-being of the parents and their extant family and of the prospective child. In an ideal world, such a process might be easy, but we do not live in an ideal world. Pregnancy often takes place outside wedlock or an alternative nurturing environment rather than within it. Young women far too young and immature to become parents find themselves pregnant. In the summer of this writing, a ten-year-old girl in Ohio became pregnant through rape. Some like her may be the victims of sexual violence. Some have simply been careless or made bad choices. Married couples may discover that they cannot either emotionally or financially care for another child. Couples in congregations I have served have discovered within the process of the pregnancy that the fetus was damaged in such a way that life would either be impossible or exceedingly difficult outside the womb. Such situations are real, not infrequent, and often tragic. But they are not situations in which the fetus has or should be assigned independent status before viability. Instead, society should trust prospective parents with the advice of their physicians to make the best decisions possible for all concerned. That decision may be abortion. It may be adoption. It may well be to give the fetus a chance for life outside the womb regardless of the difficulty entailed in making that happen. But the decision cannot be made responsibly or appropriately by anyone but those most intimately involved.

In other words, I contend that before viability, the state has no place in decisions regarding such a personal matter as abortion. That assertion points to the fundamental flaw in the Supreme Court's decision overturning *Roe v. Wade*. In essence, the court argued that the right to privacy asserted in the Fourteenth Amendment does not extend beyond those matters specifically mentioned in its text. They therefore assert that these matters should be left to the state and federal legislative bodies to decide. In effect, by opening the right to abortion to the decision of legislative bodies, the Court takes away what *Roe v. Wade* had made settled law. It reinserts the legislative branch into the private lives of American families. I would contend on the other hand that *agape* demands those decisions should be left to those best equipped to handle them—the parents, with the assistance of their medical and spiritual advisers. It really is nobody else's business.

This fundamental right to privacy that *Roe v. Wade* declared to be inherent in the Fourteenth Amendment has become the focal point at which both religious and political interests in the prospective life of the fetus is akin to God's interest in protecting and maintaining the prerogative of creation. In the last few years, through church doctrine and a number of state legislatures, abortion opponents argue that, in effect, the state's interest in protecting the life of the fetus supersedes and takes precedence over the life of the mother and the choices of both the prospective parents and the medical community. At this juncture, only the ballot box appears to have any prospect of bringing this debate to resolution in America.

Questions for Discussion and Reflection

1. Abortion is one of those ethical issues on which most people have an opinion. That opinion may come from religious background or personal experience or from the experience of a friend or family member. As of 2023, surveys suggest that somewhere around 61 percent of American adults "mostly support abortion rights."[8] Where do you come down as the discussion begins?

2. Is your opinion regarding the right to abortion primarily religious or political or some combination of the two? What role should the state play in a woman's decision whether or not to terminate a pregnancy at fifteen weeks? Twenty-four weeks? Thirty weeks? Should the answer to this question change as a pregnancy progresses?

---

8. Domenico Montanaro, "Poll: Americans want abortion restrictions, but not as far as red states are going," April 26, 2023, NPR.org, npr.org/2023/04/26/1171863775/poll-americans-want-abortion-restrictions-but-not-as-far-as-red-states-are-going.

3. Within Judeo-Christian tradition, various answers are given as to when life begins. Some faiths leave the responsibility for fetal life in the hands of the parents and their physician until birth. Some consider the fetus to be a discrete life of equal value to the mother and requiring legal protection from the moment of conception. Given this book's commitment to *agape* as a guiding ethical principle, when do you think fetal life becomes worthy of full protection?

4. Many would argue that the Bible itself has been both used and abused historically in the conversations regarding abortion. There is no specific biblical prohibition of abortion as such. What biblical values do you believe come into play here and why?

Chapter 6

Seeking Right Solutions for Climate Change

As with many other issues in twenty-first-century America, we remain divided with regard to an appropriate and faithful response to the challenge of climate change. The Roman Catholic Church laid down a marker in 2015 with Pope Francis's encyclical *Laudate Si*. In it the Pope put the challenges in terms of God's injunction to Adam in Genesis to "fill the earth and subdue it" (Gen 1:28). He challenged faithful Catholics to take up the cause of protecting and preserving the earth as God's gift to humankind. It's our responsibility to nurture the earth and pass it along unharmed to future generations. Similarly, mainline Protestant denominations in the United States have taken up the cause of environmentalism, calling on individuals, businesses, and governments to work toward such pro-environmental policies as a "carbon neutral" stance in both industry and private life. In American government, the Democratic party has tended to support pro-environment policy changes while the Republican party has tended to oppose them by arguing that they are harmful to American businesses and jobs.

At first glance, this would not necessarily seem to be an issue that should divide Christians. Either the climate is changing or it is not, and, if it is, sensible people of whatever political party or religious persuasion ought to find it in their own interests to do whatever must be done to avoid potentially catastrophic change to climate conditions. Unfortunately, like many other issues in contemporary American life, climate change has gotten caught up in the perennial battles between right and left in politics and between progressives and conservatives in Christian circles. Without getting too deeply into the weeds of who says what, this chapter will attempt to sketch in broad terms the basic arguments put forward by both sides of this debate and focus us back toward Christ's commandment to practice *agape* love as a way to move forward in the ongoing conversation.

What do Christians say when they oppose working to alleviate climate change? The argument appears to be based largely on a particular view of Christian history. In the branch of evangelicalism in which I was raised, for example, we spent almost no time or energy learning about creation care, but we spent a great deal of time and energy learning an essentially apocalyptic view of history. This present world, the story goes, is wholly evil and destined to be destroyed in a cataclysmic climax to history when Jesus comes again to rule a redeemed world in person. At that point, essentially, earth and heaven will become one, with God living among the redeemed while the remainder of humankind is consigned to hell.

This apocalyptic view of history is rooted in a literal approach to a few cryptic words from Jesus and to the Revelation to John in the New Testament and the book of Ezekiel in the Old. Unfortunately, much of this interpretation of

Scripture is rooted in an anachronistic misunderstanding of ancient literature, which Jesus and his contemporaries would have known well.

Basically, these passages reflect a poetic and often fanciful style of writing known as apocalyptic literature. Apocalyptic literature is perhaps most closely akin to modern poetry or even to science fiction. In essence, it attempts to convey deeper truth by using highly figurative imagery that is not intended to be taken literally by the reader. Those who understand this type of literature tend to suggest that the author of the Revelation to John was not attempting to say exactly what would happen historically in the future but rather to reassure persecuted Christians in his day that God would indeed bring them through their persecutions into better days. He could not say in plain terms that Rome would be defeated in its persecution of the Church, because that would have infuriated the authorities and made the persecution worse. So, he talked of the beast from the sea and the horsemen of the apocalypse. The point of the book was essentially, "Things may be terrible now, but stay faithful! In the end God wins!"

Because apocalyptic literature has been and continues to be so poorly understood by much of the church, however, the more literal interpretations of the texts have sparked elaborate attempts to predict exactly when Jesus will come again and exactly how the final battle against the world and the Devil might take place. These interpretations have often gone to encyclopedic volumes of text and given rise to cottage industries of those who claim to have discovered the "correct" interpretation of precisely what every sentence in the apocalyptic texts means for Christians today. From generation to generation, conservative Christians in this tradition have chosen to believe that the final battle between good and evil was approaching in their time. They have defined the

Antichrist, the villain in the piece, as everyone from Adolf Hitler to Barack Obama.

Note that this latter point has allowed a modern corruption of the implied political interpretation inherent in the Revelation to John. The Apostle took a political reality and spoke about it in fantastic imagery in order to provide hope to Christians in the midst of persecution. In the twenty-first century, apocalyptic Christianity attempts to make every politician who is unpopular in right-wing political circles an embodiment of the Antichrist for our own day. This move has the effect both of securing conservative Christian votes for right-wing causes and of encouraging Christians to ignore the real scientific and political realities that challenge the future of life on this planet.

By doing this, many evangelical Christians in America have adopted a view of reality that essentially takes a "throw-away" perspective toward this present world. It's "doomed." It's "evil." And, therefore, we Christians need not worry about events such as floods and fires that others might take as evidence of climate change. And we certainly don't need to worry about attempting to prevent such events or mitigate the conditions that create them. These are merely signs that the end times are approaching, when Jesus will come to transform this present "unredeemed" world into the ultimate paradise of eternity. In essence, indifference to the fate of this present world becomes an act of faith. "Jesus will protect me."

Note its practical effect, however. This narrative feeds into and supports the efforts of fossil fuel companies, producers of internal combustion engines, and others who make money from all forms of environmental pollution to argue that present global warming is merely a cyclical swing in the climate pendulum, which will soon give way to cooling as the pendulum moves in the other direction. In American politics, the Republican Party, conservative Christianity, and advocates for traditional industry have made common cause in seeking to oppose efforts to rethink America's approach to climate change, reduce pollution, and join with governments around the world to move toward sustainable, renewable practices in energy production, government, and industry.

There is a counternarrative supported by progressive Protestants and the Roman Catholic Church, both of which downplay the idea of an imminent second coming of Christ that brings an end to human history. In this more world-affirming theology, creation is a good gift from God to be nurtured, protected, and cared for. Christ "comes again" for each of us at the moment of our death, but any apocalyptic end of history is essentially ignored in favor of the church's task, given to us by God in Genesis 1 and 2, to work for the betterment of ourselves, one another, and this present world. In this view, in which faith and science are allies, our responsibility is to learn to understand creation and the challenges human activity presents to it, and to work to alleviate those challenges by whatever means necessary.

We come again to the two essential commandments given to us by Jesus. In Mark's version of the story, "The first is, 'Hear, O Israel: the Lord our God, the Lord is one; you shall love the Lord your God with all your heart, and with all your soul, and with all your mind, and with all your strength.' The second is this, 'You shall love your neighbor as yourself'" (Mark 12:29-31, NRSV). These commandments are both spiritual and worldly. Loving God necessarily includes loving God with both our mind and our strength. Since God is the author of creation in Christian cosmology, loving God entails using both our minds and our actions to love God's creation. In fact, we cannot authentically love God without also loving the world God has given us. In precisely the same fashion, loving our neighbors as we love ourselves involves wanting and working for good both for ourselves and for others. We cannot do that without working for such practical worldly things as clean air, clean water, sustainable food production, and energy sources that work with the realities of the earth, our fellow creatures, and the climate we have been given rather than depleting those resources. These are the things all humankind needs to survive and to flourish.

In effect, I would argue, as clearly as in any specific issue we have discussed so far, this one requires faithful, biblically loyal Christians to come down actively and strongly in support of ethical affirmations and governmental policies that work to minimize, and as much as possible eliminate, human damage to the natural environment. God's good gift of creation is to be cherished, protected, and nurtured as much as is humanly possible. That is the task we have been given. That is the right thing to do.

A pertinent example is unfolding now as the western United States seeks to deal with the effects of a prolonged drought and its impact on rapid development, burgeoning population, and thirsty agriculture across the region. At present the Colorado River basin provides water for more than forty million people from the Rocky Mountains to the Pacific coast. Water rights in the basin are governed by an archaic series of "first come, first served" agreements among the states in the region. They often leave out the Indigenous peoples who were here first. And they seem to prioritize the needs of both agriculture and urban development.

The difficulty for the region is that, even in good years, the water supply is severely limited by the realities of precipitation and ground water availability in an arid and semi-arid environment. There simply isn't enough water for the region to continue to grow unchecked. Indeed, if the drought continues, as it may well do, there may not be enough water for the people, farms, and industries already here. Dealing with this scarcity will require all people of good will in the region to engage together in a concerted effort to transform the way we conserve and use our limited water resources.

What might that look like? At the government level, it might involve a complete renegotiation of how water is allocated to the various constituencies of the region. States, counties, and cities may need to develop new policies for commercial, industrial, and residential water usage. It could also involve scientific search for new technologies and/or new sources of water. At the individual level, it may involve conscious effort to take responsibility for and to husband our own water usage. My wife and I, for example, live on a typical suburban lot of about 6,000 square feet. We have a forty-year-old sprinkler system, and roughly two-thirds of our yard is grass. We love our green lawn. But we're engaged right now in the process of rethinking how we minimize our water usage going forward as an act of working for the well-being of our community.

Similar conversations need to occur in a variety of areas, from minimizing global warming to conserving scarce resources to imagining how we can preserve the beauty and health of creation's gifts for ourselves and those who come after us.

Questions for Discussion and Reflection

1. At this juncture, climate change, particularly global warming, seems to be a demonstrable fact of human life on earth. The scientific community is nearly unanimous that this is so. At the same time, changes of weather from year to year and decade to decade have always been a factor in the human experience. What responsibility do people of good will have to address the dangers inherent in significant climate change?

2. In the text of this chapter, we mentioned the assertion by some sections of the Christian churches that history is rapidly approaching the return of Christ, which renders any Christian responsibility for addressing the threats of climate change unnecessary and irrelevant. Is that interpretation of Scripture a part of your own tradition? How would you respectfully engage in dialogue with someone who held a different position from your own on this interpretation?

3. In various parts of the American West, the increasing scarcity of water combined with rapid population growth and industrial development means that we are rapidly reaching the limit of nature's ability to provide the resources needed for continued growth. Should this be seen as a religious or political issue, or both?

4. How do you think climate change's stress on everyday resources such as energy, food, and water can and should be addressed by people of good will in their personal and family lives as we move toward the middle of the twenty-first century?

Chapter 7

Searching for Right and Wrong Regarding Homosexuality

Perhaps no issue in contemporary America except the role of women has divided American Christianity more for the past half-century than the question of whether homosexuality is an acceptable lifestyle for Christians. The issue plays out in both secular and parochial venues. In secular settings, Christians find themselves required to deal with political questions such as whether homosexual marriage should be treated equally with heterosexual marriage in law and in society. In essence, this is a question of privacy. Do consenting adults have the right to conduct their private lives in the way they see fit? In parochial settings, religious communions must decide whether gay people may participate equally with heterosexuals in church life and leadership. This is a question of morality and of biblical interpretation. Does the scriptural witness define homosexual conduct as inherently immoral and therefore disqualifying for church membership and/or leadership?

As with the other issues we have examined in this book, questions regarding sexuality seem to divide American politics and religion right down the middle. For example, the Roman Catholic Church has traditionally attempted to deal with these questions by adopting a kind of "yes, but" approach. Yes, gay people are to be welcomed into the church as equal and beloved children of God, they say. But homosexual conduct is condemned as immoral by Scripture and tradition. Therefore, the conclusion is that homosexual activity and marriage are prohibited. Gay people who are active sexually may not be priests or teach in Catholic schools. The church defends vigorously its right to draw such distinctions.

Similarly, Protestant denominations have struggled for years over whether and how to welcome and include gay people into church life and leadership. More liberal communions such as the United Church of Christ and the Episcopal Church have been willing for some years to bless gay marriages and to allow gays in committed relationships to serve as clergy whether state laws legalized such marriages or not. Other mainline Protestants have moved toward acceptance more slowly and in a number of cases with considerable controversy. The PCUSA, for example, voted to authorize gay marriages in 2014, but that vote resulted in the departure of a number of more conservative congregations from the denomination and in the formation of the more traditional PCA. The United Methodist Church is in the process of splitting into liberal and conservative communions around sexuality as this chapter is being written. With a more congregational polity, the American Baptist Churches have said in their biennial resolutions that "Homosexuality is incompatible with Christian practice." At the same time, individual congregations have often welcomed gay members and occasionally gay clergy without necessarily running afoul of denominational oversight. Interestingly, Peter Gomes, a gay American Baptist clergyman, adopted a Protestant version of the Roman Catholic position. As chaplain of Harvard University Chapel, he came out but remained celibate. Southern Baptists, on the other hand, continue to "disfellowship" local congregations that accept gay members.

In 2015, the US Supreme Court entered the controversy from a secular point of view in its decision *Obergefell v. Hodges*. The decision held that the equal protection and right to privacy clauses of the Fourteenth Amendment required that gay marriages be legalized and recognized as equal with heterosexual marriages in all fifty states. While the 2022 decision *Dobbs v. Jackson Women's Health Organization*, which overturned *Roe v. Wade* on the question of the right to abortion, calls into question the durability of the right to privacy in American law, the court has yet to rule on whether it will overturn marriage equality in the United States. Meanwhile, an effort to codify gay marriage as legal nationally has passed and been signed by President Biden.

The question for contemporary Christians is twofold. Are twenty-first-century Christians compelled to accept as authoritative those Scriptures that apparently condemn homosexual behavior? And, whether they personally approve of homosexuality or not, are Christians required to accept and support the right of others to enter into homosexual relationships? Volumes have been written on these topics. I cannot hope in these brief pages to explore the subject adequately. What I can do is point us back toward some first principles as filters for thinking about these questions.

First, it is essential for present-day believers who want to interpret Scripture appropriately to remember the vast historical differences that separate us from the biblical world. The biblical world was neither unintelligent nor unsophisticated, but it was largely prescientific in the modern sense. Today we understand much of human behavior as heavily influenced both by genetics and psychosocial factors. These influences don't eliminate our responsibility for the various choices we make in life, but they do often help explain why we do the things we do. Many gay people today maintain that their orientation toward same-sex relationships existed in their earliest memories. Others will say that they discovered themselves to be gay later in life. It is essential not to dismiss or invalidate people's descriptions of their perceptions of their own reality.

This contemporary perspective runs headlong into both Old and New Testament condemnations of homosexual behavior. Those condemnations can neither be dismissed out of hand nor minimized. They are present in the Levitical codes in the Pentateuch. They are also present in the New Testament, particularly in the epistles of Paul, though not in the teachings of Jesus. They express the boundaries for what was considered moral behavior both in the tribal world of the Hebrews and in the first-century world in which Paul lived and wrote. It is important, however, to remember that they focused on behavior rather than individual nature. They helped separate the monotheistic Hebrews from the pagan peoples around them. The idea of a homosexual nature was not a medical or psychological concept at the time.

In effect, contemporary Christians who take biblical condemnations of homosexual behavior as authoritative are uncritically accepting the worldview of the biblical authors. To do so, which Christians often do whenever they take particular Scriptures literally, fails to take seriously the historical context in which the Scriptures were written. It ignores the fundamental principle of biblical interpretation that suggests we must understand the context in which a Scripture was written and the audience for which it was intended if we are to understand what validity it has for us today.

To use a less fraught example, as a seminary professor, I often required my students to write a paper analyzing whether the Levitical prohibition of tattoos remains in effect for believers today. Many of them, given contemporary fashion, already sported tattoos when they received the assignment. They came from a variety of denominations ranging from very liberal to ultra conservative. I found it highly surprising that almost none of them ever felt compelled to argue that the Levitical prohibition applies to Christians today. Yet that prohibition was part of the same Levitical code that condemned homosexual behavior. They never seemed to recognize a contradiction of any kind in taking one piece of the Levitical code literally and rejecting another entirely. An Old Testament scholar, as I've suggested above, would tend to say that much of that code was intended to help the Hebrews maintain their identity as a people and differentiate themselves from tribes around them.

The question for modern biblical exegetes then becomes whether these biblical prohibitions serve a continuing positive purpose in Christian life today. To answer that, we need to look honestly at the role the church's condemnations of homosexuality have played in Western culture. Again, we do so in terms of Jesus's commandment to practice *agape* defined as willing and working for the well-being of others and ourselves. Conservative Christians argue that homosexuality in and of itself constitutes a perversion of the heterosexual nature intended for humans by God with the creation of male and female. The argument seems to be that, if all humans were living in accordance with God's will, all would be heterosexual, and there would be no homosexuality at all.

That argument, however, flies in the face of reality. Despite the church's diligent efforts through history to label homosexuals as devils or witches or the worst possible sinners, gay people have continued to be born and to recognize themselves as such, regardless of whether it was ever safe to say so out loud. In those efforts, the church has usually been joined by and cooperated in the efforts of civil government to outlaw homosexual behavior as a danger to society and to make the lives of gay people as difficult as possible.

It has only been since the second half of the twentieth century that biological and psychological research has begun to recognize that homosexuality, as far as we can determine, appears to be an innate psychosocial condition that seems to find its origin in genetic predispositions established during gestation and confirmed in early childhood development.

And it is virtually immune to alteration. More than half a century of efforts to "cure" gay people through aversion treatments, psychological therapy, chemical castration, and religious conversion have proven largely fruitless. Often, they have proven only to exacerbate self-hatred in patients and to lead to profound depression and despair. Suicide remains endemic among young gay people, though there has been some improvement in recent years as societal acceptance of gay people has grown. Still, though, the debate over what is right and wrong in the church's attitude toward gay people continues to rage, confusing the church's witness, siphoning its energy in seemingly unending conflict, and leaving generations of young people—gay, straight, or unsure of their identity—with the conviction that whatever the church has to offer is definitely not for them.

Let's look a bit more closely at Paul's mentions of homosexual behavior. In Romans 1:25-27, Paul argues that homosexuality is a natural result of humans worshiping idols, "the creature rather than the Creator." He does not say specifically what the consequence of receiving "in their own persons the due penalty for their error" is, unless he is referring to receptive anal intercourse as a sign of degradation. In 1 Corinthians 6:9, Paul uses two Greek words that specifically refer to aspects of homosexual behavior. The first, *malakoi*, can mean soft or effeminate, or it can refer to male prostitutes. It suggests the receptive partner in anal intercourse. The second term, *arsenokoitai*, is a Greek rendering of the Levitical term for a man "who lies with a man as with a woman." It suggests the active partner in anal intercourse. Taken at face value, these verses seem without doubt to condemn homosexual behavior.

More modern interpreters, however, point out that, as with biblical passages regarding the subordination of women, these passages may be heavily culturally conditioned. Paul is neither aware of nor talking about people who are naturally homosexual in their orientation. Rather, they argue, he refers to what he observes of people who are either exploited by or exploiting others. Some current interpreters argue that it is abuse and not sexuality that Paul is addressing. Indeed, it was not until modern biology and psychology began to research the origins of homosexuality that science began to conclude that a percentage of humankind are simply homosexual by nature and that to consider them sick or evil has to be seen as a perversion of God's intention for these people in creation.

If, indeed, the best of twenty-first-century psychology and biology are to be believed, then applying Christ's standard of *agape* to people who identify as gay has to mean not demanding that they change but rather helping them to become the most fulfilled people they can be within the context of their identity. This does not alter Christian standards of fidelity in relationships, but it does mean those standards now apply in the context of homosexual relationships in the same way they apply to heterosexual relations.

While contemporary interpretations of biblical standards regarding homosexuality remain quite controversial within the church, however, the secular world has moved significantly in the direction of accepting homosexual relationships as a normal part of modern life. That raises a second ethical question that Christians must consider whatever their personal beliefs may be. That is the issue of the right to privacy. In this sense, both abortion and homosexuality have found a degree of protection in the United States under the Fourteenth Amendment to the Constitution, which has been interpreted as protecting an individual's right to privacy. With regard to abortion, the right to privacy suggests that a woman's decisions about her own healthcare, including any pregnancy, is a matter for her, her family, and her medical adviser. With regard to sexuality, the right to privacy is taken to mean that adults have the right to form whatever mutually consensual relationships they may choose without interference from others or, indeed, from the state.

The 2022 Supreme Court decision *Dobbs v. Jackson Women's Health Organization*, however, struck down *Roe v. Wade*'s 1973 ruling that the right to privacy guarantees a woman's right to abortion in the United States. The court suggested that the Fourteenth Amendment may not extend the right to privacy to matters not explicitly mentioned within the text of the amendment. Justice Thomas even suggested the Court might revisit whether the right to privacy extended to homosexuality.

That decision leaves American Christians with an additional ethical question to answer: regardless of our own convictions regarding personal matters such as abortion or sexual relations, do we as Christians have the right to impose our convictions on others by dent of secular law? Can Christians rightly control someone's decision of whether to terminate a pregnancy? Or can Christians who believe the Bible condemns homosexual behavior rightly deny those who identify as homosexuals the right to the same legal and societal protections heterosexuals enjoy? In December 2022, bipartisan majorities in Congress found a compromise on this issue by requiring that a gay marriage legal in one state must be accepted as also legal in other states, even if those states do not conduct gay marriages themselves. The legislation was signed by President Biden and has yet to face legal challenges as I write.

Baptists have traditionally held that each believer is ultimately responsible for their own relationship with God as a matter of personal conscience (Phil 2:12). Believing that Paul's injunction to "work out your own salvation with fear and trembling" allows for personal freedom, they have never required that all believers must agree on every point of doctrine or behavior. Instead, they have allowed for a certain freedom of conscience even within the church. This freedom in religious conscience, I would argue, is analogous to the political right to privacy implied in the Fourteenth Amendment. In other words, in a free society, some aspects of individual life must be left up to individuals to determine for themselves. In this sense, working for the well-being of others has to include allowing them the freedom to decide for themselves how they will shape their lives and relationships. It should also include supporting and protecting their right to do so. We do this both because we should support others' freedom and because we expect others to support our own freedom to live as we choose. This is the essence both of democratic society and of Christian conscience.

We come back in conclusion to the question of whether homosexual relationships are right or wrong before God. I would argue that our best understanding of God's good work of creation is that some people, for whatever biological or psychosocial reason, have always believed and will always believe that they are gay. We must see them as "how God made them," and we must support their journey toward self-fulfillment just as we would ask them to support our own. However, even if we believe they are wrong in this self-perception, we must still support their right to live in terms of their own best understanding. That includes participation in the church. Anything else would be less than Christian.

Questions for Discussion and Reflection

1. Have you personally known homosexual people within your family or friendship circle? How would you describe their experience of attempting to live authentically as people of good will?

2. Perhaps no single issue in the last quarter-century has been more divisive for American churches than the issue of homosexuality. Why do you think this is so?

3. United Methodists are currently in the process of dividing over whether it is appropriate to bless homosexual marriages or ordain gay clergy. Does the increasing legal acceptance of homosexual rights and the continuing medical and psychological research suggesting homosexuality is an innate developmental and genetic condition compel Christians to rethink their approach to the issue? Why? Why not?

4. Homosexuality and abortion are often linked in current ethical and legal discussions as examples of the appropriate limits of political solutions to matters of personal privacy. As a Christian, is anyone else's sexuality your business? If so, how and why?

5. How should people of good will educate our children regarding sexuality?

Chapter 8

Jesus and Gun Violence

I first encountered the issue of Christians and gun control as a pastor in Louisville, Kentucky, in the 1990s. Congress had just passed a ten-year ban on the sale of most assault weapons in the United States, and the question of how to further reduce gun violence was occupying national attention. Our congregation held meetings and even got our representative in Congress to stop by and speak, but it quickly became apparent that the country had little appetite at that point for instituting further restrictions. There were plenty of other challenges to face, and we turned our attention elsewhere. Most American Christians participated uncritically at least to some degree in supporting the Second Amendment's "right to keep and bear arms." It wasn't until the second Bush administration allowed the assault weapons ban to expire and the proliferation of gun sales in the nation was succeeded by a subsequent explosion of gun violence that public attention began to turn once again to the issue.

The mass shooting at the Sandy Hook Elementary School in Connecticut on December 14, 2012, once again riveted the nation's attention on the question of how to address the growing problem of mass shootings. From that horrible week more than a decade ago until the equally horrible shooting at Robb Elementary School in Uvalde, Texas, the week before school let out for summer 2022, the nation has endured an epidemic of gun violence in schools, churches, malls, and public events that has seemed only to grow worse with the years. In the four months between January and May 2023, there were *134* victims (fatal and wounded) of gun violence on K–12 school property in the United States.[9] At first glance one would think any responsible adult, not to mention any committed Christian, would be strongly in favor of taking every possible measure to end this plague on America's sense of safety. But such is not the case.

The forces that continue to maintain gun violence as a structural part of American civil society are complex and deeply intertwined with American identity. From a secular perspective, as a nation born from revolution, Americans tend to see ourselves as needing a populace capable of bearing arms in order to protect and preserve our freedom. The Second Amendment was added to the Constitution to prevent any future ruler from doing to us what George III of England had attempted, taking away our ability to defend ourselves from oppression. The amendment reads, "A well-regulated militia being necessary to the security of a free state, the right of the people to keep and bear arms shall not be infringed." That amendment was written at the close of the eighteenth century. Arms in that setting consisted of cannons, muzzle-loaded muskets, and pistols. It took about a minute, at least, to load and fire one bullet. The framers of the amendment knew nothing of the destructive capabilities of the weapons that an ambitious military and gun industry would eventually produce.

---

9. "All Shootings at Schools from 1970–Present," K–12 School Shooting Database, k12ssdb.org/all-shootings (accessed June 7, 2023).

At the same time, America's self-identity as a frontier nation constantly expanding to the West created a gun culture heavily focused on self-reliance and the need for individual weapons for law enforcement, self-protection, and the procurement of food for one's family. The "Wild West," the repeating rifle, and handguns such as the Colt 45 captured American imagination. Even the movie industry from its earliest days has continuously fostered the ideal of the armed hero triumphantly fighting off the bad guys, be they Nazis, train robbers, Native Americans, or big-city gang members.

Christians participate in this American identity as much as anyone else in America does. Nothing in my own religious background, or, I suspect, in that of most Protestants, left us with obvious meaningful tools with which to address the question of how to regulate gun possession and/or limit gun violence in the face of American culture. My family were and still are hunters. Deer season in Arkansas qualifies as a quasi-religious ritual. Young boys are often given a .22-caliber rifle or even a full-size one as soon as they are able to hold and aim it. At one point when our son was a teenager, the Methodist youth group leaders in our city offered shooting lessons to the members! And the National Rifle Association together with the gun manufacturers and the Republican Party have done a masterful job in convincing many Americans, including devout Christians, that the Second Amendment guarantees the right to unfettered access for all Americans to any weapon they have the money to purchase without restrictions. In essence, gun rights advocates take the last few words of the amendment, "shall not be infringed," quite literally and ignore both the context in which it was written and the claim in the amendment itself that it is intended to foster a "well-regulated militia."

The question is what approach should Christians take to a challenge like gun violence? Biblical guidance is minimal.

Guns hadn't been dreamed of yet. In the Old Testament God appears to take sides in human conflicts, to bless some and curse others. This reflects the primitive understanding of tribal peoples, and it can often be quite brutal. The prophet Isaiah does appear to recognize the limits of brute strength: "Woe to those . . . who trust in chariots because they are many and in horsemen because they are very strong . . ." (Isa 31:1, NRSV). And in the New Testament, Jesus specifically rejects the weapon of the day for his followers: "Then Jesus said to him, 'Put your sword back into its place, for all who take the sword will perish by the sword'" (Matt 26:52).

Today's Christians, however, live in a different world. Our responsibility is to take the values of Jesus as we are taught in the Gospels and extrapolate them for our own day. In this sense, *agape* is infinitely adaptable. Willing and working for the well-being of ourselves and others requires that we put aside whatever prejudices we may hold regarding an issue and take a clear-eyed look at how to create the greatest good for the greatest number.

Note before we move forward, though, that we are not discussing the military or matters of national defense here. We have already in chapter 3 alluded to Just War Theory and its place in human geopolitical conflicts. Issues related specifically to pacifism as a Christian lifestyle are also outside the scope of this discussion. What we are attempting to do is to create for American Christians and others of good will an ethical approach consistent with Jesus's teachings that helps us think about how guns are manufactured, bought, sold, and used within the context of American civil society. We are doing so in the context of a society that has considerably more guns than it has people. We are doing so in what is arguably the most violent society in the developed world. The United States has more guns, more murders, more mass shootings, and more deaths in the course of a year from gun violence than any other society on the planet. The question in the face of this appalling reality is, "What can we realistically do?"

It is essential to recognize that the myth of unlimited gun ownership in the United States as an absolute constitutional right is just that, a myth. The Second Amendment was added to the Constitution for the specific purpose of allowing the nation to construct what we today call our National Guard. The Guard is a corps of part-time citizen soldiers in every community who are available for the civil authorities to call out in case of emergency threats to civil order. The amendment does also protect the right of individuals to own personal weapons, but it does not suggest or imagine that this right should be absolute. The purpose of the amendment is civil order, "the general welfare," as the Preamble to the Constitution states. It cannot be properly used for purposes that abuse or degrade the general welfare.

In the interest of the general welfare, gun ownership and use can be regulated in ways appropriate to maintaining order and creating a general ethic of gun safety. This ethic can and should include a number of precautions.

First, all guns sold should be licensed and registered in a national database so that weapons used in crimes can be confiscated and destroyed. We would not imagine allowing anyone in the United States to own and drive an unlicensed vehicle. Gun licensing should be no different. All those who wish to purchase a gun for any purpose should first have to pass a test akin to a driving test in which they demonstrate they understand proper use and storage of their weapon. And they should be required to report any prospective weapon sale so that the new owner can pass their own test and secure a new license for the weapon.

Second, gun sales to the public should be regulated to require as a part of the licensing process that people

seeking to buy weapons be screened in advance through a national criminal database. That database needs to be computerized at a state-of-the-art level. All state and local jurisdictions should be required to participate in keeping the database updated and current. Individuals flagged by police, medical professionals, or their own families as having a previous history of criminal behavior or tendencies toward violence should have to undergo further examination before they are allowed to purchase or to continue to hold a weapon.

Third, only handguns, sporting rifle, and hunting rifles should be available for purchase and ownership by the general public. Military-style weapons of any kind should be available only to the National Guard and to local, state, and national public safety officers. They should be allowed to hold such weapons for the duration of their service only. All military-style weapons currently in public hands should be repurchased at public expense and destroyed. All multi-round magazines should be illegal to sell to or to be owned by civilians. And computer-printed guns should be subject to exactly the same regulations as commercially manufactured weapons.

A careful reader will notice that, whereas in all the previous topics I have considered in this book, I have suggested that Christians could reasonably take views contrary or even antithetical to one another, I have not done so here. My rationale is simple and, I profoundly hope, Christian. *Agape* as Christ commanded us requires us to will and to work for the well-being of ourselves and others. Guns kill and injure people. That is why they were invented. Except for hunting for food for sport or for self-protection, that is their only reason to exist or to be tolerated in civil society. We will not begin to be safer as a society until and unless we develop the moral and political will to reject our mythologies and acknowledge as a nation the profound damage our current gun policies do to our society, our families, and our children every day.

Questions for Discussion and Reflection

1. In this chapter, the author takes several specific policy positions regarding gun violence in America. Is he correct that the urgency and universality of this problem in the United States require people of good will to work at every level of society to find ways to address the issue?

2. Scripture can't specifically address gun violence simply because guns hadn't been invented when the Bible was written. Yet the Scriptures strongly renounce resorting to violence as a means of settling human problems. And there have always been communions that have made pacifism an aspect of their faith. Historians say it was the church's acceptance as the official church of the Roman empire that led to a practical compromise between church and state in such doctrines as Just War Theory. Is it time to revisit Christian values and positions with regard to violence?

3. The proliferation of guns in America has led to a growing fear of gun violence on the part of many Americans. Some choose to purchase and learn to use personal weapons as a potential means of protection for themselves and their families. Others want no part of personal gun ownership. What are the relevant pros and cons in this discussion, and where do religious values enter the conversation?

4. Do you think guns have become so much a part of American culture that nothing practical can be done to reduce gun violence in our society? If you could implement one specific policy that you think would make our society safer, what would that policy be, and how would you go about getting it done?

Chapter 9

A Way Forward

The real question is whether the way of decision-making I'm suggesting proves durable for American Christians specifically and people of good will generally as we move forward into the challenges ahead. How might we apply the approach to issues as they arise? Here are some guidelines I've found useful.

I approach issues by drawing on faith and reason. To do that, I'm guided by a handful of assumptions:

• For people of faith this approach will work better if one believes that God is good and that God loves us and wants the best for us and calls us to work toward that best future together. For those who are not people of faith the approach must be tied to a philosophical concept of active benevolence as a basis for living.

• At the same time, God will not rescue us from our own bad choices. We are allowed to live out the consequences of whatever decisions we make. No meaningful faith or philosophical perspective allows human beings to take harmful actions without consequence.

• Science is our friend, and we must remain willing to learn from and apply the lessons it teaches us about what is happening both in the physical world and in human interactions as understood by the medical and social sciences.

• There is a sense in which every solution is tentative and provisional. It is tentative because circumstances may or may not allow our preferred solution to be implemented. And it is provisional because there may be unforeseen consequences to what we choose or we may learn new information that makes our solution incomplete or outdated.

We need to make every effort possible to approach the challenges we face in an organized and thorough fashion. In other words, ethical solutions in a complicated world require an approach, a methodology. We need to think carefully about what we do and how we do it. What I want to do as we finish this little book is suggest a way we can all go about approaching the ethical issues we'll no doubt encounter in the future. Every problem is different. But once we have found ourselves with a problem to be solved, we can outline logically the steps or movements in ethical decisions that people of faith and/or good will are likely to follow.

1. In attempting to solve a problem, we always begin from our own lived experience. I told you a bit about my own background as we began partly because I wanted you to know something of the experiences and perceptions I bring to making decisions and partly because I want you to get in the habit of thinking carefully about the experiences and convictions that shape your own approach to every issue you face. It makes a difference whether you grew up poor or rich, white or Black or Hispanic or Asian or Native American. Rural folk often value nature and the environment differently from those who grew up in the city. Within Christianity, people who grew up mainline or evangelical Protestant or Roman Catholic or Orthodox often have different worldviews, as do people who grew up outside the church and convert as adults and people who grew up in the church but reject organized religion as adults. People from other faith traditions or none at all bring their unique experiences to the process of making decisions as well.

Simply put, you and I have to know where to begin. One way to do that is to ask ourselves, "When it comes to right and wrong, where do I get my beliefs?" The answer to that question will tell you a great deal about the biases you may bring to any difficult decision. It reminds me, for example, that my childhood histories of racism, assumed white privilege, fundamentalist religion, and southern tribalism are always there in the background for me no matter how much I may think that I have thoroughly left them behind. If you can't articulate those background biases for yourself, they will undoubtedly taint your decision-making process in ways you do not anticipate.

2. From lived experience we then move to our own current ethical ideals. In short, what kind of people do you and I intend and want to be? We all have what might be called default motivations in our day-to-day lives. If we're in this life for the money we can make or the number of sexual partners we can have, those motivations will undoubtedly govern our ethical decisions. In contemporary politics, for example, observers will argue that either or both parties have left guiding principles behind in a single-minded pursuit of raw power. The truth is that lesser motives will always in some degree taint human decision-making. We do not live in a perfect world.

If, though, we move forward in a consistent pursuit of "wanting and working for the well-being of ourselves and others," as I have suggested is an appropriate translation of *agape*, that opens us up to explore what might be appropriate solutions in regard to particular issues. In addition to *agape*, it's appropriate for Christians to ask what other biblical principles might apply in a given situation.

This, however, is precisely the point at which many Christians falter in their consideration of contemporary issues. It is undoubtedly true that the Bible contains a wide variety of prohibitions, prescriptions, and pronouncements on a whole host of issues. Because Christians have always made a great deal of loyalty to Scripture as a basic tenet of the faith (the historic fights over "biblical inerrancy" are a prime example of this), many feel disloyal or even heretical when modern science or psychology leads them to question a biblical prohibition. When this happens, it is vital to remember, first, that the Bible is a human book, written as many generations of believers sought to understand what God's spirit was teaching them in a wide variety of disparate historical situations.

That means, second, that what was true and appropriate for believers in one era of history may not be so for believers today and in the future. Scientific understanding has vastly progressed since the canon was formed in the fourth century. Viewing scientific progress as God's good gift and a fulfillment of God's command in Genesis to "till the earth and subdue it," contemporary believers need not hesitate to suggest that biblical "absolutes" based on imperfect understandings don't have to continue to be absolutes today. We must always be open to the possibility that God is telling us it's time to change our minds!

3. The third step in considering any issue must therefore consist in attempting to gather the best possible information we can find. What are the facts regarding this issue? Whom will be affected by treating it one way or another? How do we balance the legitimate claims of the interests of the majority versus the equally legitimate aspirations of a minority? We live in a contentious era when what are considered the facts regarding a given question may vary considerably depending on the perspective of the one answering the question. The facts regarding American

immigration policy, for example, will appear different to a
farmer in the Rio Grande Valley attempting to protect her
land from constant encroachment by asylum seekers and
those same asylum seekers standing on the south bank of
the river viewing the US as a "promised land" offering them
freedom and security from the violence in their country of
origin.

Nonetheless, the responsibility of a decision-maker is to
do their honest best to consider all the relevant data at their
command as they seek to process an issue. They must also, as
much as possible, be honest with themselves as they consider
the data points of their own selfish interests and prejudices.
As someone, for example, who lives close to the headwaters of
the Colorado River, I have the water rights interests of Colorado as an inherent bias. But I must also realize that Utah,
Arizona, Nevada, California, Mexico, and the native peoples
of the Colorado basin have competing interests and claims
upon the river's water. In addition, the long-term well-being
of the Colorado valley ecosystem, quite apart from human
claims, has to be considered.

It's especially important to check information for its
source of origin and its reliability. It's also important to be
reluctant to accept any source of information that we cannot
verify. Misinformation, especially online and through broad-
cast media, has become as endemic as Covid and often even
more vicious. As I've been working on this chapter, for
example, Paul Pelosi, husband of Congresswoman Nancy
Pelosi, was hospitalized after being viciously attacked by an
intruder in his own home. In less than twelve hours, rumors
began to circulate online suggesting that he had some sort of
previous relationship with the attacker. These were entirely
false, and the head of the San Francisco Police Department
went on television to say both that the rumors were false and
that dealing with that sort of misinformation from multiple

sources was seriously hampering their actual investigation. In short, do check the sources of information you acquire and do not rely on any information you cannot verify.

4. Once we have in hand the best data we can find, we can begin to move toward using that data and our own values to reach a decision on what to do. It may be best to develop a list of the data points to be considered and then, using *agape* as a filter, rank the data we have in terms of how much weight a given data point should carry in seeking to make a decision.

Necessarily, political, social, and religious factors play a role in any ethical decision you and I make. Something you may want to do may be the right thing in the abstract, but it may not be practical in your specific situation. You may well have competing claims on your time, resources, and loyalty. After looking at the current situation in Ukraine, for example, you might come to the conclusion that it would be right and good to send $5,000 to help alleviate hunger there this winter. Yet that same $5,000 might also be needed by your own family or to pay off a previously contracted debt.

Similarly, while *agape* along with biblical injunctions to help the hungry and to welcome strangers should give us a bias toward welcoming immigrants from troubled nations, there are always limits on the structures and resources we have available to do so. In other words, efforts to be a welcoming society must be organized in such a way that we can help as many people as possible without becoming overwhelmed by a level of demands we cannot meet. That does not change our values or commitments. It simply recognizes reality.

For people of faith, this process of prioritization as we move toward a decision will inevitably include seeking guidance from the divine. In many religious traditions, prayer, meditation, and contemplation have an important place in making decisions among alternate courses of action. For

Christians, this process means seeking the guidance of the Holy Spirit. That guidance is necessarily deeply personal and subjective. It is a data point only in the most immeasurable sense. Yet believers will often affirm that this piece of the process is ultimately determinative in the way they choose to act on any ethical issue.

5. The fifth step in making an ethical decision is then to take appropriate action. Action in this sense may be short term or long term. It may be a specific deed to take a stand or help an individual or a group of people. It may be an effort to begin educating ourselves and others on an issue. It may involve voting for a particular party or even choosing a candidate from a party different from your own. This is what we usually think of when we think of ethics in a contemporary context. Or the action we take may be a longer-term change such as a change in our own attitudes or actions toward a group of people or a specific societal problem. Climate change, as we are experiencing it globally in the early twenty-first century, is a long-term issue for the survival of the planet. It did not happen overnight, and it will not go away quickly or as a result of a single action or attitude. Any genuine solution to the issue will require a determined change of mind and a multitude of actions by a host of different actors around the globe. As I write, this year's international climate initiative meeting has just taken place. As usual, many nations participated and others did not. Getting the kind of universal global commitment necessary to meet the challenge is considered by many to be an urgent matter of survival. But no nation and no individual actor or group can do this alone. Like many other ethical issues in our day, it may seem completely overwhelming.

Yet, as with any ethical issue, the most vital thing is to begin. On the day she refused to move to the back of the bus in Montgomery, Alabama, Rosa Parks likely never dreamed she was sparking a movement that would change the face of American society. She just did what she could do that day on that bus. She began. Similarly, no matter the issue, people of good will are called to do what we see that we can do. We are called to begin.

6. The sixth step is to evaluate whether what we have done has achieved or is likely to achieve the result we desired. Sometimes what we believe to be the correct ethical action will have unforeseen consequences that work against the goals we have in mind. At other times, our chosen course of action may need a course correction or adjustment to be optimally effective. In the real world, ethical actions are seldom flawless, and that means people of good will must be open to continual growth and change as we pursue what we believe to be worthy goals. Sometimes we need to change our actions in order to achieve the goal we want. Sometimes the actions we take will teach us by their result that what we really need to do is change our goal.

The interesting part of this evaluative process is that it isn't usually all that difficult to realize that the action we've taken isn't working. The hard part is to understand why our course of action isn't working and what we can do to change it. Because change is difficult, we're often tempted to keep doing what we've been doing even when we know it isn't working. And yet the oft-repeated axiom that the definition of insanity is to keep doing what we've been doing and expect a different result comes into play here. To attempt to live ethically, to find the difference between right and wrong and live rightly, is to open oneself to continual reevaluation and change.

7. The final step in the decision-making process thus involves forgiving both oneself and others for past mistakes and choosing a new course of action to replace the one you've found to be inadequate. In Christian terms, this is the process of receiving grace. But that process is not merely valid for Christians; it is also a vital element in general human interactions. As long as we hold on to blame against ourselves or others, that blame becomes an obstacle that can often block progress in our actions. Only by refusing to let past enmities and offenses govern our present actions can we hope to move forward.

I'm aware that this assertion may come across to some as either moralistic, impossibly pious, or simply a naïve and impractical way to look at the world. But I do not believe it to be any of those things. Some wag is supposed to have said, "In romantic love the unforgivable sin is a good memory." If they really did, I think the saying applies to ethical progress as well. When the native Africans in South Africa finally managed to take political power there, they could have embarked on a long effort to punish those who had championed apartheid and spent so many years oppressing their native peoples. But they didn't. Led by Anglican Bishop Desmond Tutu, they instead embarked on a process of national reconciliation. They didn't hide what had been done. They invited those who had been the oppressed and those who had been the oppressors to meet together, be honest about what had happened, and ask and receive forgiveness. It took years. It wasn't easy. It wasn't perfect. But it began to weave hopeful threads of community and common purpose between Black and white South Africans too long divided and distrustful of one another. I include this seventh step in the process to say that in ethics, it's crucial never to give up on ourselves and never to give up on one another.

In the end, you see, at almost every level, addressing ethical issues productively requires maintaining good personal relationships. Spending twenty years as a pastor of four different local congregations across the country, I learned that the best lubricant for maintaining productive relationships is to be willing to apologize, forgive and ask forgiveness, and come at a problem again from a new perspective. I often apologized for a perceived slight even if I didn't necessarily think I'd done something wrong. Apologies did wonders for soothing feelings and allowing people to move forward together toward a productive solution. And more often than not, offering an apology myself allowed the other person the emotional room they needed to apologize to me!

There you have it, a seven-step process for addressing issues of right and wrong as we move forward in this first half of the twenty-first century. For those who visualize better with a diagram, I include one to help you see how this process can hang together. After all, no primer is complete without a diagram!

How to Process an Ethical Issue

1. State the problem

↓

2. Consider your background

↓

3 Examine your ideals

↓

4. Gather relevant data

↓

5. Prioritize data according to ideals

↓

6. Take appropriate action

↓

7. Evaluate whether the action is producing the desired result

↓

8. Move toward a new statement of the problem and a revised course of action)

Questions for Discussion and Reflection

1. What do you see as the strengths and weaknesses of the decision-making technique outlined above? In what ways do you think it could or could not work for you in making future decisions?

2. If you come from a perspective other than faith-based, how would you go about adapting the assertions in this book for your own ethical purposes? Would they work or not? If not, what standards would you prefer?

Sample Sermon

I preached the following sermon in the First Presbyterian Church of Fort Collins, Colorado, on January 29, 2023.

When You're Not Sure about the Bible

John 16:12-13

Do you ever feel you have to choose between what the Bible says and what you think is right? These days those of us who want to be faithful followers of Jesus sometimes feel backed into a corner. Do we use our heads, paying attention to science and education and our own beliefs about how we ought to live in the world and treat other people? Or do we choose obedience to words of Scripture that sometimes feel to us as though they were written very long ago and very far away? Not only that, a careful reading shows us that the Bible itself is sometimes contradictory. In the Old Testament, for example, God often appears to be telling the Hebrews that the only way to faithfully follow Yahweh is to kill all the heathen. In effect, wipe them off the face of the earth. But in the New Testament, Jesus tells us the way to get rid of the heathen is not to destroy them but to help them. "Go ye therefore and make disciples of all."

The problem is how you and I are supposed to distinguish between biblical teachings that still apply and situations where the Spirit of Christ has changed or wants to change our minds. We begin with our text from John's Gospel.

It's Jesus's last evening with the disciples. He's talking with them about how to go on following him once he's no longer here physically, and he says, "I still have many things to say to you but you cannot bear them now. When the Spirit of truth comes, he will guide you into all the truth, for he will not speak on his own but will speak whatever he hears, and he will declare to you the things that are to come."

Think about that with me for a minute. Many of us have been raised to believe that the Scriptures are God's last, final, and only word on how to live our lives. But what Jesus is telling us is, "I'm not finished with you yet. I have a lot more to say. And the Spirit is going to tell you what." The Scottish preacher and commentator William Barclay says it this way: "Revelation is progressive."[10] One of the reasons I really like these verses in John is they help us answer people who want to argue that a two-thousand-year-old religion can't possibly have anything to say to you and me and our real-world problems here in the twenty-first century. The answer is it's not two thousand years old. The message of Easter is that Jesus is alive not dead. He's not gone. He's here. Through the Holy Spirit, he's right here in Fort Collins, Colorado, on this last Sunday morning in January 2023. Our faith only started when Jesus physically walked the earth. From the day he ascended to this day, the Holy Spirit has continued to teach

---

10. *The Gospel of John*, Daily Bible Study Series, vol. 2, rev. ed. (Philadelphia: Westminster, 1976), 194.

us the things Jesus didn't have time or opportunity to teach us while he was here.

Take slavery, for example. When Jesus walked the earth, somewhere around one out of every three people in the Roman Empire lived as a slave, powerless human property. As early as his letter to the slave owner Philemon, Paul starts to say, "Wait a minute. If your slave becomes a Christian, how can you still treat him as property? Isn't that slave your brother now?" It took a long time for that lesson to sink in. As late as the lead-up to the Civil War, slave owners were still using the Bible to justify our modern version of slavery. "They held slaves in the Bible," the plantation preachers said. "When Onesimus became a Christian, Paul sent him back to his owner." That's right as far as it goes. Paul did send him back. But he also made it impossible for Philemon to ever look at Onesimus in the same way again. Paul planted a seed the Spirit cultivated and fertilized through the centuries till it became impossible for slavery to survive as a legitimate part of any Christian society. And clearly, from what happened in Memphis this month, we still have more to learn.[11]

So our first point today, my sisters and brothers (every sermon ought to have at least one point, and this is today's first!), is "Revelation is progressive." God's not finished with us yet. Christ through the Holy Spirit is still changing you and me and believers everywhere. That's the first point.

And here's the second. In 2023, much of the Christian journey does still involve preserving and passing on what Jesus has taught us so far. The Bible is still authoritative for our faith because it's where we learn who Jesus was when he walked the earth, all that he said and did and showed us by his life and death and resurrection. You and I can spend much

---

11. This sermon was written after a recording of police fatally beating Tyre Nichols, a Black man, was widely distributed across television and the internet.

of a lifetime letting the Scriptures speak to us and change us because the Spirit still speaks to us through them. Talking about today's passage, theologian Gail O'Day writes that much of the faith is and always has to be about conserving what we've been given.[12] That's the second point. It's short because it's what most of us have always believed anyway.

But here's the third point. Because of what Jesus says here in John, you and I dare not stop with what Scripture says. Beyond learning the Bible, the rest of your journey and mine consists of learning and putting into practice what Jesus through the Spirit is still teaching us. In other words, you and I have to go on changing our minds.

Let's explore that a little bit. For many of us, especially those of us over fifty, changing our minds is hard. We grow up learning to think a certain way and do things a certain way, and that way of living becomes our culture. Take driving for example. We drive on the right-hand side of the road. Sheryl and I love road trips. We take them all the time. And we drive on the right all the way there and back. We like road trips. But the first time we went to England and rented a car, we got a terrible shock. The steering wheel was on the right. The gear shift was left of the wheel. And then we had to drive on the left. To make it worse, they invented traffic circles. They call them roundabouts. You enter on the left; you go left around them, and if you don't keep to the left you never ever get out. I'm frankly surprised I'm not still in one. Change is hard.

But from the moment God told us to learn how to till the earth and keep it, changing and growing has always been a part of God's plan for you and me. For a long, long time, Christian culture acted as though God's giving the earth to us

---

12. *John*, The New Interpreter's Bible: A Commentary in Twelve Volumes (Nashville: Abingdon, 1995), 777.

meant we could do anything we wanted to with it. And we did. Generations of farmers, ranchers, and property developers across the West prospered by digging deep wells for irrigation and drinking water through damming rivers and building reservoirs. But now the underground aquifers are being depleted and prolonged droughts are drying up our rivers and reservoirs. And we have to learn how to make our water demands appropriate for a thirsty land. A similar process of depletion has happened with oceans and fisheries. We're learning to our sorrow that the planet has limits. We can only change the content of the air around us so much before we end up changing the weather. The sober truth is that God's not going to fix these things for us. We have to learn how to fix them ourselves. But the good news is that God's Spirit is still here, still working with you and me, if we want to, to build a better world for ourselves and all God's creation.

Fourth, God wants to work with you and me to make things better. Science and religion are not enemies. God gave us science so we can learn how to take care of ourselves and creation. So what do we do when life or science or modern society make us want to change or go beyond or even contradict what some part of Scripture tells us?

Fifth, we do our best to model what we say and do and how we treat God's world and God's creatures and especially one another by who Jesus is and what Jesus does. When he tells us to love God with all our heart, mind, and soul and to love others as ourselves, he isn't being sentimental. He is giving us a template to guide us as we walk through the world. My old Christian ethics professor used to say the *agape* kind of love Jesus is talking about means to will and to work for the well-being of those we love. To will and to work for their well-being. Sometimes that is simple. And sometimes it's incredibly complex. Sometimes a crying baby just needs a diaper change or a hungry child needs a peanut butter sand-wich. Sometimes the world needs a new vaccine or a town needs a better road through a canyon without destroying the beauty of God's creation. Sometimes your spouse just needs a hug, or you just need one yourself. And sometimes an entire group such as our African American sisters and brothers, or those refugees fleeing violence in other parts of the world, or people whose gender identity or orientation is outside our comfortable traditional stereotypes needs us to rethink and even discard old prejudices or outmoded beliefs and ways of doing things, even if they are somewhere in Scripture. Whether you and I need to change the way we think or change the way we act, the journey of our lives as followers of Jesus is to let him teach us how to love well. There's a meme going around on the internet that my wife Sheryl shared with me that sums this up pretty well. Listen carefully and you'll see what I mean.

"Genocide is biblical. Loving your enemy is biblical. But only one is Christlike. Slavery is biblical. Chain breaking is biblical. But only one is Christlike. Patriarchy is biblical. Counter-cultural elevation of women is biblical. But only one is Christlike. Retributive violence is biblical. Grace-filled restoration is biblical. But only one is Christlike. Segregation is biblical. Unity is biblical. But only one is Christlike. Christ, not the Bible, transforms. Be wary of those who know one but not the other."

To put it another way, my sisters and brothers, the Bible is not our God. We study it but we don't worship it. We worship Jesus.

So what do we do? We follow Jesus. We ask ourselves what really is the loving thing to do. Given the best we know and the best we're able to understand about whatever the issue is, what works for the well-being of others and ourselves even if that's not what some verse of the Bible says? We never stop learning. And that is what we do. In the name of the Father and of the Son and of the Holy Spirit. Amen.

About the Author

Ron Sisk retired in 2015 as emeritus professor of homiletics and Christian ministry from Sioux Falls Seminary, Sioux Falls, South Dakota. He also served that institution for six years as academic vice president and dean. Before beginning his seminary service in 2002, he served for twenty years as pastor of four Baptist churches in Kentucky, California, and Texas. He began his post seminary career in 1982 as director of program development at the Christian Life Commission of the Southern Baptist Convention. His ordination is recognized by the American Baptist Churches. He is the author of numerous articles and sermons and three previous monographs. He is married to Sheryl and has one son, Douglas.

www.ingramcontent.com/pod-product-compliance
Lightning Source LLC
LaVergne TN
LVHW051600080426
835510LV00020B/3065

Advance Praise for *Right and Wrong*

In this brief, highly readable book, Ron Sisk defines a Christian approach to contemporary ethical issues that works. His selected topics and discussion prompts make the book useful for individual and group study. Chapter 9 alone is worth the price of the book!

—*Rev. Dr. Michael Smith*
Retired Pastor, Editor, and Writer
Knoxville, Tennessee

At a time when the church and its leaders are navigating ever more polarizing political and cultural landscapes, we all need this "ethical" road map more than ever. Ron boldly addresses some of the most crucial social and theological challenges of our day through the wise, thoughtful, and faithful lens of Christian ethics. More important than agreeing or disagreeing with any views shared in this book, the reader is invited into honest reflection and then left with a clear framework for continuing their own discernment. This book is a timely gift to the church and Christ's disciples.

—*Rev. Dr. Corey Nelson*
Pastor, First Presbyterian Church of Fort Collins

Ron Sisk is right. We have lost our way in discerning right from wrong, truth from falsehood. This book points to a practical, rational, balanced way forward. It is a timely, practical, and necessary guide for our time.

—*Dr. Loyd Allen*
Emeritus Professor
McAfee School of Theology, Mercer University

How can we give our best response to the complex moral issues that confront us? Ron Sisk's book *Right and Wrong* gives us a thoughtful way forward. Though I don't agree with all he proposes, I do benefit from having engaged the rigors of his easy-to-read book.

—Leslie Hollon, PhD
Baptist Pastor, Ecumenical Leader, Traveler

Deeply learned yet remarkably accessible, this primer by a seasoned Christian ethicist and pastor Ron Sisk charts a focused *agape* pathway in a morally confusing epoch. He writes with perceptiveness in our religiously plural context, offering the admonition that "intelligence, science, curiosity, [and willingness] to work with the Holy Spirit" is the right approach. I recommend this as a constructive offering to adult faith formation groups, theological students, and all who seek helpful moral guidance in our fraught times.

—Dr. Molly T. Marshall
President, United Theological Seminary of the Twin Cities

If you like to think, read, and have conversations about current issues and Christian moral values, I recommend Ron Sisk's new pandemic memoir, *Right and Wrong: Finding Values for the 21st Century*. Sisk, a retired pastor and seminary ethics professor, wrote this book during the Covid pandemic as he was thinking about the connections between crucial social issues and making ethical decisions from a progressive Christian perspective. He brings his training in political science, American social history, and Christian ethics to his work with biblical interpretation, church, and culture.

Each chapter ends with questions for personal reflection and group conversations. I believe these conversations and studies will be most productive with people and in groups that have the knowledge, vocabulary, experience, and maturity that produce healthy discussions and fruitful actions.

—Ray Higgins
Retired Seminary Ethics Professor, Pastor, and
CBF Arkansas Executive Coordinator